WORSHIP through the CHRISTIAN YEAR

All-age resources for the *Common Worship* lectionary

YEAR C

edited by Diana Murrie and Hamish Bruce

Contributors:
Gill Ambrose
Graham Barrett
Isobel Booth-Clibborn
Joan Chapman
Jenny Hyson
Steve Pearce
Betty Pedley
Judith Sadler
Robin Sharples

The National Society
*Leading Education
with a Christian Purpose*
Church House Publishing

National Society/Church House Publishing
Church House
Great Smith Street
London SW1P 3NZ

ISBN 0 7151 4890 7

Published 1997 by the National Society (Church of England) for Promoting Religious Education and Church House Publishing

First impression with corrections 2000

Printed in England by The Cromwell Press Ltd

Contents

Appendix A

Collects and Post Communion Prayers: Ordinary Time (Before Lent)

Appendix B

Collects and Post Communion Prayers: Ordinary Time (After Trinity and Before Advent)

Acknowledgements

The publisher gratefully acknowledges permission to reproduce copyright material in this book. Every effort has been made to trace and contact copyright holders. If there are any inadvertent omissions we apologize to those concerned and undertake to include suitable acknowledgements in all future editions.

C   =   Collect
PC   =   Post communion prayer

The Archbishops' Council: pp. 16–17 (C and PC), 51 (PC); 54 (C), 57 (PC), 58 (C), 60 (C), 63 (PC), 118 (C), 122 (C), 126 (C), 131 (C: Third Sunday after Trinity), 133 (C: Ninth Sunday after Trinity), 134 (C: Thirteenth and Fourteenth Sundays after Trinity), 135 (PC: Sixteenth Sunday after Trinity; C: Seventeenth Sunday after Trinity), 136 (C: Eighteenth Sunday after Trinity), from *The Alternative Service Book 1980*; pp. 64 (C), 130 (PC), 132 (PC), from *Lent, Holy Week, Easter*, 1984 and 1986; pp. 12 (C), 21 (PC), 25 (PC), 29 (PC), 121 (PC), 130 (PC: First Sunday after Trinity), from *The Promise of His Glory*, 1991; pp. 65, 75, 85 123, 133 (PC: Ninth Sunday after Trinity), 136 (PC: Nineteenth Sunday after Trinity), from *Patterns for Worship*, 1995; pp. 40 (C), 55 (PC), 128 (C: Fifth Sunday before Lent), from *The Prayer Book as Proposed in 1928*; pp. 23 (PC), 129 (PC: Third Sunday before Lent), 136 (C: Twentieth Sunday after Trinity); 137 (PC: Twenty-First Sunday after Trinity), by the Liturgical Commission.

Ateliers et Presses de Taizé, 71250 Taizé Community, France: p. 43, from *Music from Taizé* Vol.2 HarperCollins 1985.

Stephen Brown: p. 13, from Donald Hilton (ed.), *Seasons and Celebrations*, NCEC, 1996.

Cambridge University Press: pp. 6 (C), 8 (C), 10 (C), 14 (C), 19 (PC), 20 (C), 30 (C), 42 (C), 44 (c), 45 (PC), 47 (PC), 52 (C), 56 (C), 62 (C), 66 (C), 68 (C), 70 (C), 116 (C), 120 (C), 124 (C), 127 (PC), 128 (C and PC: Fourth Sunday before Lent), 129 (C), 130 (C: First and Second Sundays after Trinity), 131 (C: Fourth and Fifth Sundays after Trinity; PC: Fifth Sunday after Trinity), 132 (C: Sixth, Seventh and Eighth Sundays after Trinity), 133 (C: Tenth and Eleventh Sundays after Trinity), 134 (C: Twelfth Sunday after Trinity), 135 (C: Sixteenth Sunday after Trinity; PC: Fifteenth and Seventeenth Sundays after Trinity), 136 (C: Nineteenth Sunday after Trinity), 137 (C: Twenty-first Sunday and Last Sunday after Trinity). Extracts adapted from *The Book of Common Prayer* (1662), the rights in which are vested in the Crown, are reproduced by permission of the Crown's Patentee, Cambridge University Press.

The Continuum International Publishing Group Ltd: pp. 9 (PC), 28 (C), 39 (PC), 134 (PC: Thirteenth Sunday after Trinity), 135 (C: Fifteenth Sunday after Trinity), 136 (PC: Twentieth Sunday after Trinity), from David Silk (ed.), *Prayers for Use at the Alternative Services*, 1980; revised 1986; pp. 125 (PC: Second Sunday before Advent), 133 (PC: Eleventh Sunday after Trinity), from C. L. MacDonnell, *After Communion*, 1985. Copyright © Mowbray, an imprint of Cassell.

Church of the Province of Southern Africa: pp. 24 (C), 26 (C), 50 (C), 123 (PC), from *An Anglican Prayer Book*, 1989 © Provincial Trustees of the Church of the Province of Southern Africa.

The Consultation on Common Texts: *The Revised Common Lectionary* is copyright © The Consultation on Common Texts 1992. The Church of England adaptations to the Principal Service lectionary are copyright © The Central Board of Finance of the Church of England, as are the Second and Third Service lectionaries.

Emmanuel Church, Northwood: p. 29, from Michael Perry (ed.), *Church Family Worship*, Hodder & Stoughton, 1986.

Episcopal Church of the USA: p. 46 (C), from *The Book of Common Prayer* according to the use of the Episcopal Church of the USA, 1979. The ECUSA Prayer Book is not subject to copyright.

General Synod of the Anglican Church of Canada: pp. 9 (PC), 15 (PC), 27 (PC), 41 (PC), 59 (PC), 65 (PC), 67 (PC), 69 (PC), 105 (PC), 117 (PC), 128 (PC: Fifth Sunday before Lent), 131 (PC: Fourth Sunday after Trinity), 132 (PC: Sixth Sunday after Trinity), 134 (PC: Twelfth and Fourteenth Sundays after Trinity), 137 (PC: Last Sunday after Trinity), based on (or excerpted from) *The Book of Alternative Services of the Anglican Church of Canada*, copyright © 1985. Used with permission.

General Synod of the Church of Ireland: pp. 18 (C), 53 (PC), 61 (PC), from *Alternative Prayer Book*, 1984; Collects and Post-Communion Prayers, 1995. Reproduced with permission.

Peter Graystone and Eileen Turner: pp. 79, 81, 101, from Peter Graystone and Eileen Turner, *A Church for All Ages: A Practical Approach to All-age Worship*, Scripture Union, 1993.

The Right Reverend Christopher Herbert: pp. 37, 87, from Christopher Herbert (comp.), *Prayers for Children*, NS/CHP, 1993.

Hodder & Stoughton Limited: p. 13 (PC), from Frank Colquhoun, *Parish Prayers*, 1967. Reproduced by permission of the publisher.

International Commission on English in the Liturgy: pp. 31 (PC), 136 (PC: Eighteenth Sunday after Trinity), from the English translation of *The Roman Missal*, © 1973, International Committee on English in the Liturgy, Inc. All rights reserved.

The Venerable Trevor Lloyd: p. 39, from *Liturgy and Death*, Grove Booklet 28, 1974. (also published in *Patterns for Worship*, 1995)

Janet Morley and SPCK: p. 131 (PC: Third Sunday after Trinity) from *All Desires Known*, SPCK, 1992.

National Christian Education Council: p. 57, Richard Hughes, 'Our Lord Jesus Christ, risen from death', adapted from Hazel Snashall (ed.), *When you Pray with 7–10s*, NCEC, 1983. Reproduced by permission.

Oxford University Press: pp. 22 (C), 38 (C), 71 (PC), from *The Book of Common Worship of the Church of South India*.

Canon Michael Perham: pp. 48-9 (C and PC), from Michael Perham (ed.), *Enriching the Christian Year*, SPCK/Alcuin Club, 1993.

Mrs B. Perry/Jubilate Hymns: pp. 35, 41, 93, 97, 125, from Michael Perry (ed.), *Church Family Worship*, Hodder & Stoughton, 1986.

The Right Reverend Kenneth Stevenson: 133 (PC: Tenth Sunday after Trinity).

Westcott House, Cambridge: pp. 11 (PC), 43 (PC), 119 (PC).

Wild Goose Publications: pp. 63, 77, 127, from Kathy Galloway (ed.), *The Pattern of our Days: Liturgies and Resources,* Wild Goose Publications, 1996.

Introduction

Worship through the Christian Year has been compiled to help those who design all-age learning and worship – both clergy and laity – to explore and implement the varied opportunities offered by the *Common Worship* lectionary.

For each Sunday there is a brief summary of the Old Testament, New Testament and Gospel readings, ideas for a talk or sermon, group and/or congregational activities, ideas for prayers and intercessions, stories and other resources, suggestions for songs and hymns, and the appropriate collect and post communion prayer.

The aim of the book is to stimulate an individual, creative approach. It could be that the ideas suggested here may inspire something totally different yet appropriate for your church. This is to be welcomed and encouraged. Only those working with real people in a real church can effectively identify what will, or will not be, successful in their 'patch'.

Using the *Common Worship* lectionary

The *Common Worship* lectionary is closely based on the Revised Common Lectionary that is already used by a number of other Churches throughout the world. Readings are provided for every Sunday and Holy Day in the Christian year.

Year A This focuses on the Gospel of Matthew. During Advent, the Old Testament reading is from Isaiah, illuminating the Gospel readings about the coming of Christ, and the second readings come from Romans and 1 Corinthians. From Ash Wednesday to Pentecost, while Matthew remains the focus, there are some of the traditional readings from John's Gospel, during the last three Sundays of Lent and the Easter season.

Year B This focuses on the Gospel of Mark. During Advent, the New Testament readings come mainly from the two letters to the Corinthians, while from Ash Wednesday to Pentecost the New Testament readings are a semi-continuous reading from 1 John. The first readings come from Acts during the Easter season in Year B.

Year C This focuses on the Gospel of Luke, again with readings from John coming in during the Ash Wednesday to Pentecost season. After Easter, there are semi-continuous readings from Revelation. After Pentecost, Jeremiah figures largely in the Old Testament reading, with semi-continuous selections from Galatians, Colossians, 1 & 2 Timothy, and 2 Thessalonians.

As in the other years, the final Sundays after Pentecost focus on the Second Coming and the reign of Christ.

If you are unfamiliar with the *Common Worship* lectionary, it is worth carefully reading the Notes section of *The Christian Year: Calendar, Lectionary and Collects*, CHP, 1999. This outlines a number of points that you should bear in mind as you plan the Sunday service. These are summarized below:

- When there are only two readings at the Principal Service and that service is Holy Communion, the second reading is always the Gospel reading.

- In the choice of readings other than the Gospel reading, the minister should ensure that, in any year, a balance is maintained between readings from the Old and New Testaments and that, where a particular biblical book is appointed to be read over several weeks, the choice ensures that this continuity of one book is not lost.

- Verses in brackets may be included or omitted, as desired.

Worship through the Christian Year comprises three volumes of resource material to match Years A, B and C of the lectionary.

Church Year (Advent to Advent)	Lectionary Year
1999/2000	B
2000/2001	C
2001/2002	A
2002/2003	B
2003/2004	C
2004/2005	A
2005/2006	B
2006/2007	C
2007/2008	A
2008/2009	B
2009/2010	C

The seasons of the Christian year
Advent

The Christian year traditionally begins on the First Sunday of Advent, four weeks before Christmas. The *Common Worship* lectionary returns to this pattern rather than the ASB model which begins the year on the Ninth Sunday before Christmas.

Christmas

Material has been provided for the Christmas Day service itself and for the two Sundays after Christmas.

Epiphany

This season includes material for the Epiphany (which can also be celebrated on the Second Sunday of Christmas) and for the four Sundays of Epiphany, as well as for the service celebrating the Presentation of Christ in the Temple (Candlemas) that is celebrated either on 2 February or on the Sunday falling between 28 January and 3 February.

Ordinary Time (Before Lent)

There are two periods of 'ordinary time' in the new calendar, the first being relatively short lasting from the Presentation of Christ until Shrove Tuesday. There is no seasonal emphasis in this period. Greater flexibility is given in this period to the worship leader. As is stated in the Notes to *The Christian Year: Calendar, Lectionary and Collects*: 'During Ordinary Time . . . authorized lectionary provision remains the norm but, after due consultation with the Parochial Church Council, the minister may, from time to time, depart from the lectionary provision for pastoral reasons or preaching or teaching purposes.'

The Sunday (lectionary) provisions in this shorter period of Ordinary Time are: Proper 1, Proper 2, Proper 3, The Second Sunday before Lent and The Sunday next before Lent. The first three are used for Sundays that fall in a specific period of time: Proper 1 for Sundays between 3 and 9 February inclusive, Proper 2 for Sundays between 10 and 16 February inclusive and Proper 3 for Sundays between 17 and 23 February inclusive. As the date of Easter obviously changes each year, these Propers similarly chop and change. For instance, if Easter is earlier than usual, you might only use Proper 1 and 2. This may seem confusing and it is recommended that you refer to the specific annual guides such as *Calendar, Lectionary and Collects: Advent 1999 to Advent 2000* (CHP, 1999).

To further complicate the issue, the collects during Ordinary Time are not linked with specific calendar dates, like the lectionary readings, but to the Sunday title. So in this period of Ordinary Time the collects are for the Fifth, Fourth, Third, Second and the Sunday Next before Lent. For ease of use, we have grouped all

of the collects and post communion prayers for Ordinary Time – at the back of the book in Appendix A (see pp. 128–9). Again, you will need to refer to the specific annual lectionaries to place the readings and collects together. We have provided a simple chart to show which collects and post communion prayers you should use for these services for the next three Year C lectionary years.

Lent

This period includes the five Sundays of Lent and Palm Sunday. Mothering Sunday can be celebrated in preference to the provision for the Fourth Sunday of Lent and we have concentrated on this festival in *Worship through the Christian Year*.

Easter

This season runs from Easter Day, through the Second to Seventh Sundays of Easter and culminates in Pentecost. If the Old Testament reading is used during the Sundays in Eastertide, the reading from Acts must be used as the second reading.

Ordinary Time (After Trinity)

This is a lengthy period of Ordinary Time which runs from Trinity Sunday, through Propers 4–25, ending with Bible Sunday and the Dedication Festival. As in the first period of Ordinary Time, the collects and lectionary readings do not have the same name. All dates cited are inclusive. We have again placed all the collects for this period at the end of the book (see Appendix B on p. 130).

During this period, alternative Old Testament readings are given. Those under the heading 'Continuous' offer semi-continuous reading of Old Testament texts but allow the Old Testament reading to stand independently of the other readings. Those under the heading 'Related' relate the Old Testament reading to the Gospel reading. It is not recommended that you move from week to week from one column to another. One column should be followed for the whole sequence of Sundays after Trinity.

Ordinary Time (Before Advent)

This short period rounds off the Christian Year. It begins with All Saints' Day and ends with the festival of Christ the King.

Resources

Many churches that have already spent large amounts of money on resources for children's work and all-age activities may be concerned about having to purchase a whole range of new resources to complement the new lectionary. The approach in *Worship through the Christian Year* has been to recommend books and other resources that you may already possess.

The following list is divided into core books which are referred to in a number of sessions and others which are referred to only occasionally. It may be a helpful guide to building up a library of resource material for use by all the leaders in your church. To save unnecessary repetition, only the titles of the core books are cited in each session (these are listed alphabetically by title below).

Core books and resources

All Aboard!, Steve Pearce and Diana Murrie, NCEC, 1996

Building New Bridges, Claire Gibb, NS/CHP, 1996

Celebration! Celebrating for all God's family, Margaret Withers and Tony Pinchin, Gracewing, 1996

Children and Holy Communion, Steve Pearce and Diana Murrie, NS/CHP, 1997

The Christian Year: Calendar, Lectionary and Collects, CHP, 1999

Church Family Worship, Michael Perry (ed.), Hodder & Stoughton, 1986

A Church for All Ages: A Practical Approach to All-age Worship, Peter Graystone and Eileen Turner, Scripture Union, 1993

Common Worship: Services and Prayers for the Church of England, CHP, 2000

The Discovery Wheel, Gillian Ambrose, Andrew Gear and David Green, NS/CHP, 1994

Festive Allsorts, Nicola Currie, NS/CHP, 1994

The Haffertee storybooks, Janet and John Perkins, Lion

Lent, Holy Week, Easter, CUP/SPCK/CHP, 1984 and 1986

Patterns for Worship, CHP, 1995

The Pattern of Our Days, Kathy Galloway (ed.), Wild Goose Publications, 1996

Pick and Mix, Margaret Dean (ed.), NS/CHP, 1992

Praise, Play and Paint! Jan Godfrey, NS/CHP, 1995

The Promise of His Glory, Mowbray/CHP, 1991

Seasons, Saints and Sticky Tape, Nicola Currie and Jean Thomson, NS/CHP, 1992

The stories of Teddy Horsley, Leslie Francis and Nicola Slee, NCEC

Together with Children subscription magazine, NS/CHP

Under Fives – Alive!, Jane Farley, Eileen Goddard, Judy Jarvis, NS/CHP, 1997

Other useful resources
Drama

Michael Forster, *Act One*, Kevin Mayhew, 1996

Michael Forster, *Act Two*, Kevin Mayhew, 1996

Anita Haigh, *Rap, Rhyme and Reason*, Scripture Union, 1996

Derek Haylock, *Plays for All Seasons*, NS/CHP, 1997

Derek Haylock, *Plays on the Word*, NS/CHP, 1993

Dave Hopwood, *Acting Up*, NS/CHP, 1995

Dave Hopwood, *A Fistful of Sketches*, NS/CHP, 1996

Paul Powell, *Scenes and Wonders*, NS/CHP, 1994

Ruth Tiller, *Keeping the Feast: Seasonal Dramas For All-age Worship*, Kevin Mayhew, 1995

Bible resources

Pat Alexander, *Young Puffin Book of Bible Stories*, Puffin, 1988

Arthur Baker, *Palm Tree Bible*, Palm Tree Press, 1992

Selina Hastings (ed.), *The Children's Illustrated Bible*, Dorling Kindersley, 1994

Storybooks and poetry

Jim Dainty, *Mudge, Gill and Steve*, NS/CHP, 1997

Geoffrey Duncan (ed.), *Dare to Dream*, Fount, 1995

Susan Varley, *Badger's Parting Gift*, Collins, 1984

Philip Welsh, *Ignatius Goes Fishing and More Beastly Tales*, Scripture Union, 1979

Philip Welsh, *The Reluctant Mole and Other Beastly Tales*, Scripture Union, 1979

General resource books

Mary Batchelor, *The Lion Christmas Book*, Lion, 1986

Christopher Herbert, *Prayers for Children*, NS/CHP, 1993

Gordon and Ronni Lamont, *Children Aloud!*, NS/CHP, 1997

Sue Relf, *100 Instant Children's Talks*, Kingsway, 1994

Susan Sayers, *Focus the Word*, Kevin Mayhew, 1989

Susan Sayers, *More Things to Do in Children's Worship*, Kevin Mayhew, 1996

Katie Thompson, *The Complete Children's Liturgy Book*, Kevin Mayhew, 1995

How to use this book

 ## Lectionary readings

These are the readings set for the Principal Service in Year C and provide the main ideas and thrust for the Sunday worship. The principle on which the lectionary is constructed is that the readings speak for themselves, without a stated theme. This may mean that those compiling services come up with different thematic material. That is perfectly acceptable. What is offered here are resources which tend to follow one trend or idea in the readings; these will need adjusting and selecting according to the readings and main idea which those planning the worship decide to emphasize. The following sections will have to be adapted accordingly but this should not be difficult for anyone used to designing all-age learning and worship.

 ## Talk/address/ sermon

These are designed as starting points, arising from the collect and readings. They can be used to prepare material for use in church, or for other occasions such as a school assembly. Further suggestions can be gleaned from looking at the Congregational/group activities section, as can ideas for visual aids to illustrate the talk or sermon. These can be prepared in advance, perhaps by the children and young people of the church, particularly if you have a mid-week group. It will involve them more fully in mainstream Sunday worship. But, as pointed out above, feel free to interpret or develop the readings in the way most appropriate to your situation. It would be helpful to look at the Stories and other resources section for further ideas.

 ## Congregational/ group activities

These are suggestions for activities that develop from the readings and collect. It is important that if work is produced by groups outside the main worship, the rest of the church should have the opportunity to see the results at some point. No indication has been given here as to which activities are suitable for different age groups. It is left entirely to the leaders to decide what would be appropriate. If your church has yet to experience all-age congregational activities, now could be the time to try!

 ## Prayers/ intercessions

Again, these are designed to inspire creativity and originality. It is important that anything produced in the Congregational/group activities section which could be used here should be, and that those leading these activities should be made aware of this.

 ## Stories and other resources

Resources already in use for ASB activities can be used effectively with the *Common Worship* lectionary, even session-dated material. The core books in the Resources section have been widely used by children's work leaders across the dioceses. If you do not have any, or many of them, do consult your Diocesan Children's Work Adviser about them, or inspect them in your local bookshop. It might be interesting for you to note when you last purchased a new resource book!

 ## Music

Each church tends to have its own unique mixture of songs, taken from a diverse range of music books. We have chosen a selection of songs, choruses and modern hymns, alongside familiar traditional hymns, that will help you to focus upon the lectionary readings. Again, it must be stressed that these are only *suggested* songs and hymns and do not provide a complete or definitive list. Please see page 5 for a list of music books and their abbreviations.

 ## Drama

In recent years, a number of excellent drama books have been published. We have given a few suggestions for appropriate sketches for some of the Sundays in the Christian year. Although the sketches need to be rehearsed in advance, the end result is certainly worth any extra effort.

Collects and post communion prayers

These are the set prayers for the relevant Sunday and can also be used in non-eucharistic worship. The collect for each Sunday is used on the following weekdays, except where other provision is made. *The Christian Year: Calendar, Lectionary and Collects* provides further collects for saints' days throughout the year.

Music book abbreviations

BBP   *Big Blue Planet*, Stainer & Bell and Methodist Church Division of Education and Youth, 1995

CAYP   John L. Bell, *Come All You People,* Wild Goose Publications, 1994

CCH   *The Complete Celebration Hymnal with New Songs of Celebration*, McCrimmon Publishing Company, 1984

CHE   *Celebration Hymnal for Everyone*, McCrimmon Publishing Company, 1994

CP   *Come and Praise*, Volumes 1 and 2, BBC Books, 1978

FG   *Feeling Good!*, NS/CHP, 1994

HAMNS   *Hymns Ancient and Modern New Standard*, Hymns Ancient and Modern Limited, 1983

HON   *Hymns Old and New: New Anglican Edition*, Kevin Mayhew, 1996

HTC   *Hymns for Today's Church*, Hodder & Stoughton, 1982

JP   *Junior Praise*, Marshall Pickering, 1986

JU   *Jump Up If You're Wearing Red*, NS/CHP, 1996

MP   *Mission Praise*, Marshall Pickering, 1992

MT   *Music from Taizé*, Volumes 1 and 2, HarperCollins, 1985

SHF   *Songs and Hymns of Fellowship*: Integrated Music Edition, Kingsway, 1987

SLW   *Sound of Living Waters*, Hodder & Stoughton, 1974

SS   Don Pickard and Alan Luff (eds), *Story Song*, Stainer & Bell and Methodist Church Division of Education and Youth, 1993

WGS   John L. Bell and Graham Maule, *Wild Goose Songs,* Volumes 1 and 2, Wild Goose Publications, 1987, 1988

WP   *World Praise* (Music edition), HarperCollins, 1993

The First Sunday of Advent

 ## Readings

Jeremiah 33.14-16

The prophet writes about the coming of a deliverer or Messiah for the Jewish people, who will save the nations of Israel and Judah. He will be a descendant of King David.

1 Thessalonians 3.9-13

Paul prays for the people of Thessalonika and looks forward to being with them again so that he can help them prepare for the coming again of Jesus. This is one of many references in Paul's writing to the Second Coming of Jesus which was an important focus for the earliest Christians. Advent has traditionally been the season when Christians prepare themselves to meet Jesus.

Luke 21.25-36

In the previous passage, Luke describes Jesus speaking about the destruction of the Temple and the coming destruction of Jerusalem. Here he describes the signs that will show that the Son of man is coming to deliver his people and bring in the kingdom of God. He urges everyone to look for the signs, to pray and make ready for the time when the Son of man will appear. Luke's message is one of hope for a people experiencing persecution as Jesus himself did. The Son of man will bring them freedom. They must be ready for him.

Collect

Almighty God,
give us grace to cast away the works of darkness
and to put on the armour of light,
now in the time of this mortal life,
in which your Son Jesus Christ
    came to us in great humility;
that on the last day,
when he shall come again in his glorious majesty
    to judge the living and the dead,
we may rise to the life immortal;
through him who is alive and reigns with you,
in the unity of the Holy Spirit,
one God, now and for ever.

 ## Talk/address/ sermon

Take in an Advent calendar to show at the beginning of the talk.

Advent means coming. Advent is a time of preparation, a time of waiting with Advent calendars and the Advent Wreath. But this can become simply counting of days.

How do we prepare ourselves for the coming of Christ? It depends on what we expect of his coming.

Jeremiah writes of deliverance from oppression. Paul writes of Christ's Second Coming, and the Gospel passage emphasizes the need to be ready for the kingdom of God. The readings suggest that we are waiting for one who will make an enormous difference. What do we perceive the difference to be?

 ## Congregational/ group activities

- Make an Advent Wreath: use three purple candles and one pink one for the outside ring with a white one in the centre. Light the first purple candle when the Gospel is read. Purple is the traditional colour of Advent and Lent – symbolizing our longing for forgiveness – and this colour should be used for the First, Second and Fourth Sundays of Advent

- Make Advent triangles (see diagram on opposite page). Draw an equilateral triangle with 23 cm sides onto strong bright paper or thin card. Divide it into four triangles internally. Draw tabs on each side. Lightly score the internal lines and edges where the tabs will bend. Choose one internal triangle (this will become one face of the solid triangle when it is finally constructed) to work on. Choose two phrases from the Gospel to write in the triangle: perhaps 'Be alert. The kingdom of God is near.' Decorate the rest of the space with silver stars and the sun and moon. Keep the triangles carefully until next week.

- Begin to make a Jesse Tree. Use a dead branch secured firmly in a pot. Draw and cut out the figure of Jesse asleep and place him at the base, fixing King David to the trunk of the tree just above him, as the Old Testament reading is read. Everyone can add the buds of the fig tree onto its branches after the Gospel reading. Decorate the pot with the words 'I will fulfil the promise I made to the house of Israel and the house of Judah' and the sun, moon and stars and the ocean waves of the Gospel reading.

- The people of Israel hoped for a Messiah to deliver them from foreign oppressors. Discuss in groups the ways in which peoples of the world are oppressed today, how they might be freed from their oppression and what we can do to bring the day of their freedom closer. Note responses and place these, with Advent candles of hope, in some dark corner of the church. Stand around the candles for the prayers of intercession.

Prayers/ intercessions

Assemble the congregation around the Advent candles of hope that were described in the previous activity. Use the following response:

Leader   Maranatha.

All   **Come, Lord Jesus.**

(The Aramaic word 'Maranatha' means 'Our Lord, come'.)

The responsive intercessions for Advent printed on page 66 of *Patterns for Worship* are particularly suitable for use today.

Stories and other resources

Baboushka: a traditional Russian story, retold in *The Lion Christmas Book*, Mary Batchelor, Lion, 1986

Douglas Clark, 'Hope for the children', in *Dare to Dream*, Fount, 1995

The Advent sections in *The Discovery Wheel* (p. 10), *The Promise of His Glory* (p. 91) and *Seasons, Saints and Sticky Tape* (p. 5)

Drama

Paul Powell, 'Nearly ready', in *Scenes and Wonders*, NS/CHP, 1994

Ruth Tiller, 'Countdown', in *Keeping the Feast*, Kevin Mayhew, 1995

Music

Come, Lord Jesus, come (BBP 29, JU p. 88 – perhaps just the first verse this week)

Wait for the Lord (HON 528, MT2 p. 78)

Maranatha – Veni Domine (MT1 p. 79)

Prepare the way (SHF 457)

When he comes (SHF 599)

Come, thou long-expected Jesus (HAMNS 31, HON 98, HTC 52)

Thy kingdom come, O God (HAMNS 177, HTC 335)

Jesus shall reign (HAMNS 143, HTC 516)

Post communion prayer

O Lord our God,
make us watchful and keep us faithful
as we await the coming of your Son our Lord;
that, when he shall appear,
he may not find us sleeping in sin
but active in his service
and joyful in his praise;
through Jesus Christ our Lord.

The Second Sunday of Advent

Readings

Baruch 5.1-9

In this passage the writer is offering hope to the Jews exiled after the fall of Jerusalem. He describes how they will return to Jerusalem and God's splendour will be shown.

or

Malachi 3.1-4

An awesome messenger will prepare the way for the Lord to return to the Temple. God's people will be purified so that they may respond to him as they did in ancient times.

Philippians 1.3-11

Paul is looking forward to the day of Christ: the day when the redemption of the world is so complete that Christ will appear in glory to hand over the kingdom to his Father. With joy, Paul prays that the people of Philippi who have shared in his suffering will live in a way that will prepare them for this day.

Luke 3.1-6

John, the son of Zechariah and cousin of Jesus, calls for repentance and uses the beautiful words of the prophet Isaiah, asking people to prepare for the coming of the Lord who will save his people. This passage serves to link the sparse details of Jesus' childhood with the beginning of his adult ministry, John the preacher fulfilling the prophecies of Isaiah, his father Zechariah and with the angel Gabriel's message that he will prepare a way for the Lord.

Collect

O Lord, raise up, we pray, your power
and come among us,
and with great might succour us;
that whereas, through our sins and wickedness
we are grievously hindered
in running the race that is set before us,
your bountiful grace and mercy
may speedily help and deliver us;
through Jesus Christ your Son our Lord,
to whom with you and the Holy Spirit,
be honour and glory, now and for ever.

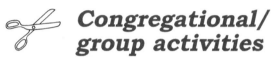 Talk/address/ sermon

Why do the prophets describe salvation with such extravagance – the levelling of mountains, the glorious entry to Jerusalem, and so on? Today it is matched by the glories of preparation for the mid-winter festival – extravagant lights and decorated shopping centres. Yet these simply vanish with the sales bargains at the beginning of January. How do we ensure that the glorious message of salvation is more than a dose of mid-winter comfort?

Congregational/ group activities

- Light the first and second purple candles on the Advent Wreath. Sing the first and second verses ('Lord we need you now') of 'Come, Lord Jesus, come' (JU p. 88).

- Decorate the second face of the Advent triangle: write on it the words 'Prepare a way for the Lord, make his paths straight' and decorate it with a picture suggested by the words of Baruch 5.7–9 (a straight path through the hills and forests).

- Read together the passage from Malachi and then do some cleaning. Clean some dirty silver with silver polish, or use soap and water to rub clean a piece of really dirty fabric, or rub clean some dirty coins using brass cleaner. (Use plastic gloves when using chemicals with children.) If you happen to know a jeweller, you could arrange with them an opportunity to demonstrate the melting of gold or silver or how they clean dirty metal.

- In groups, look through a wide variety of newspapers and cut out headlines which members agree show the sins of our society. Gather them together and  use them as a visual focus for an act of penitence introduced by the words of Luke 3.3.

- Give people card, pen and pebbles and ask them to design a simple board game to illustrate the words of John the Baptist from Isaiah 40.3-5.

- Add to the Jesse Tree. This week add a picture of John the Baptist and symbols associated with him – a picture of desert or modern wasteland, mountains and pathways; sandals, locusts and a honeycomb.

- In *The Voyage of the Dawn Treader* by C. S. Lewis, Eustace, who is constantly ridiculing the other children, is turned into a dragon. In Chapter 7, having learnt his lesson, he loses his skin and becomes a boy again. Summarize the story so far and read the section in which he describes the experience of having his dragon skin torn off. Talk, then, about ways in which we hide bits of ourselves that we are ashamed of from other people. What would we like to change about ourselves in order to prepare for the Lord's coming; which skins would we like to shed? Then read together the passage from Malachi.

Prayers/ intercessions

Use the following responses as thanksgivings, or in place of a song or reading:

My soul is waiting for the Lord:
in his word is my hope.
My soul is waiting for the Lord:
in his word is my hope.

Out of the depths have I called to you, O Lord.
Lord, hear my voice.
In his word is my hope.

There is forgiveness with you:
therefore you shall be feared.
In his word is my hope.

My soul is longing for the Lord,
more than those who watch for daybreak.
In his word is my hope.

O Israel, wait for the Lord,
for with the Lord there is mercy.
In his word is my hope.

Glory to the Father, and to the Son, and to the Holy Spirit.
My soul waits for the Lord:
in his word is my hope.

adapted from Psalm 130
Patterns for Worship, p. 115

Stories and other resources

C. S. Lewis, *The Voyage of the Dawn Treader*, HarperCollins, 1980 (first published 1952)

J. G. Priestley, 'A loud and angry voice', in *Bible Stories for Classroom and Assembly, the New Testament*, RMEP, 1994

'What is coming? Who is coming?', in *Celebration: Celebrating for All God's Family* (p. 88)

Drama

Derek Haylock, 'Message received but not understood', in *Plays for All Seasons*, NS/CHP, 1997

Music

Come, Lord Jesus, come (BBP 29, JU p. 88) – verses 1 and 2 this week

The ballad of the Son of man (SS 21) (selected verses)

How lovely on the mountains (SHF 176, HON 219)

For your kingdom is coming, Lord (SHF 115)

Lift up your heads (SHF 328)

Make way, make way (HON 329)

Come Holy Ghost, our hearts inspire (HAMNS 448, HTC 589)

Thou whose almighty word (HAMNS 180, HTC 506)

The advent of our King (HAMNS 25, HON 470)

Post communion prayer

Father in heaven,
who sent your Son to redeem the world
and will send him again to be our judge:
give us grace so to imitate him
in the humility and purity of his first coming
that, when he comes again,
we may be ready to greet him
with joyful love and firm faith;
through Jesus Christ our Lord.

The Third Sunday of Advent

 ## Readings

Zephaniah 3.14-20

Zephaniah wrote in a time of political turmoil and he continually calls for people to return to God's ways. This passage concludes the book with a call for the people to be joyful, for God is coming as their king. Even the weak will be rescued and all will be happy again.

Philippians 4.4-7

In this famous passage Paul encourages the people of Philippi to be joyful and thankful as they pray, for the Lord is near.

Luke 3.7-18

John the Baptist explains to those who come for baptism what is meant by repentance. He speaks to the crowd, the ordinary people, and his demands are radical. It is not their inheritance as children of Abraham that will save them but a concern for the poor and for justice. John's message attracted those on the edge of society, for he speaks to soldiers and tax collectors. His message is exciting to those who hear it but John tells them that someone even greater will follow him.

Collect

O Lord Jesus Christ,
who at your first coming sent your messenger
to prepare your way before you:
grant that the ministers and stewards of your
   mysteries
may likewise so prepare and make ready your way
by turning the hearts of the disobedient
   to the wisdom of the just,
that at your second coming to judge the world
we may be found an acceptable people in your
   sight;
for you are alive and reign with the Father
in the unity of the Holy Spirit,
one God, now and for ever.

 ## Talk/address/ sermon

How do we prepare ourselves for Christ to come? Is it simply a matter of personal preparation or is it the urgency of the world's cry for justice that should take precedence? Is there a tension between personal piety and delivering the oppressed? What must we do about it? And how does this all relate to the secular preparation for Christmas which impinges so strongly on our lives?

 ## Congregational/ group activities

- The Third Sunday of Advent is traditionally known as Gaudete Sunday. 'Gaudeo' is a Latin word meaning 'Rejoice' and refers to Philippians 4.4: 'Rejoice in the Lord always' which is part of the New Testament reading today. For this reason, we light the pink candle on the Advent Wreath today, along with the two purple ones from the previous weeks. Pink is the traditional colour for the Third Sunday of Advent as a symbol of our rejoicing as we await the coming of the Saviour. Sing 'Fill us with your peace' (the third verse of 'Come, Lord Jesus, come') which also picks up a theme of the passage. Traditionally some churches will choose to light the pink candle on the Fourth Sunday of Advent for the Annunciation.

- Decorate a third face of the Advent triangle. Write the words: 'What must we do? Be content. Share your cloak.' Decorate it with pictures suggested by the Gospel passage.

- Learn the song 'Rejoice in the Lord always' (HON 430) and sing it as a two- or four-part round. Make up a simple dance to go with it. Use it with verses of the Zephaniah reading.

- Bells have traditionally been used as a way for the Church to express its rejoicing. Invite someone to come and teach hand-bell ringing, or visit the bell tower with your bell ringers.

- Add to the Jesse Tree. Make bells from silver foil to hang on the tree. You could also add a well (representing the springs of salvation from Isaiah 12), a representation of the city of Jerusalem (Zion) and a dove of peace.

- John told ordinary people to share their tunics, soldiers not to intimidate people and tax collectors not to take more than their share. Discuss in groups what John would have asked of each of us.

- Listen to 'The Bell Anthem' by Henry Purcell. (The words are those of the New Testament reading.)

Prayers/ intercessions

Thank God for reasons to rejoice: for each other; for families and friends; for the coming of Christ and the approaching season of Christmas; for the salvation which Christ came to bring.

Use this response based on the reading from Zephaniah:

Leader   Let us shout for joy!

All   **Let us exult with all our hearts!**

Pray for those who are oppressed, exploited or intimidated; for the will to change the sins of our society. Use this response based on the Gospel reading:

Leader   Lord, help us prepare your way and make your paths straight:

All   **so all humanity may see your salvation.**

Stories and other resources

Colin Gibson, 'Let justice roll down', in *Dare to Dream*, Fount, 1995

Leonard Clark, 'Bells ringing', in David Davis (ed.), *A Single Star*, Puffin, 1976

Selina Hastings (ed.), 'John baptises Jesus', in *The Children's Illustrated Bible*, Dorling Kindersley, 1994

Katie Thompson, 'Lead lives filled with goodness' (Third Sunday of Advent Year C), in *The Complete Children's Liturgy Book*, Kevin Mayhew, 1995

'Injustice' (p. 62) and 'Repentance and Forgiveness' (p. 80) in *The Discovery Wheel*

'An act of penitence', in *The Promise of His Glory* (p. 125)

 ## Music

Come, Lord Jesus, come (BBP 29, JU p. 88) – verses 1, 2 and 3 this week

I will rejoice, I will rejoice (SHF 260)

Rejoice in the Lord always (HON 430, SHF 462)

Rejoice! (SHF 461)

Jubilate Deo (BBP 2)

Rejoice!, the Lord is King! (HAMNS 139, HON 432, HTC 180, SHF 463)

The kingdom is upon you (HAMNS 512)

Hark! a herald voice is calling (HON 196)

Post communion prayer

We give you thanks, O Lord, for these heavenly gifts;
kindle in us the fire of your Spirit
that when your Christ comes again
we may shine as lights before his face;
who is alive and reigns now and for ever.

The Fourth Sunday of Advent

 ## Readings

Micah 5.2-5a

Ephrathah (Bethlehem) is the city of David, the great king of Israel, and because of this, it is from Bethlehem that the Messiah or deliverer will come. The descent from David is also emphasized in the shepherd metaphor: the ruler will defend and care for his people as a shepherd does his sheep.

Hebrews 10.5-10

The writer quotes Psalm 40: the words are used to describe the Son coming in bodily form to do God's will. This surpasses all the offerings made to fulfil the Law, for Christ's offering is the greatest of all.

Luke 1.39-45[46-55]

Mary visits her cousin Elizabeth, who is to be the mother of John, and they praise God for the babies they are to have. John and Jesus are linked together but Elizabeth's greeting of Mary shows that Jesus is to be the greater of the two.

Collect

God our redeemer,
who prepared the Blessed Virgin Mary
to be the mother of your Son:
grant that, as she looked for his coming as our
  saviour,
so we may be ready to greet him
when he comes again as our judge;
who is alive and reigns with you,
in the unity of the Holy Spirit,
one God, now and for ever.

 ## Talk/address/ sermon

As the nativity approaches, we are directed to the family credentials of Jesus. He is to be of the house of David, born in Bethlehem, where Rachel was buried and Ruth married Boaz. He will be foreshadowed by his cousin whose mother, Elizabeth, we read of greeting Mary in this week's Gospel reading. This concern with the family lineage of Jesus reflects not only the value attributed to family life and faith in the Jewish tradition but serves also to emphasize the importance of the humanity of Jesus in the incarnation.

Congregational/ group activities

- Light all four candles on the Advent Wreath. Sing 'Touch us with your love', the fourth verse of 'Come, Lord Jesus, come' (JU p. 88).

- Decorate the fourth face of your Advent triangle. Write on it the words 'You are the most blessed of all women and blessed is the child you shall bear' and illustrate the meeting of Mary and Elizabeth. Fold the triangle along the score lines and make it into a solid shape. Glue the flaps inside and add a thread by which to hang it. Smear it with a fine coating of extra glue in places if you would like to and dust on a little glitter. Hang the triangles on the church Christmas tree or let people take them home for their own Christmas tree.

- Get out your church's crib figures and prepare them for Christmas: clean off the dust, make any repairs that are necessary. Talk about what each of the figures would have been doing in the weeks just before the birth of Jesus. Imagine what 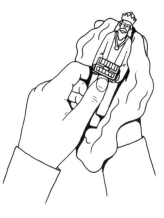 Elizabeth and Mary would have talked about while they were together and how they would have prepared for the birth of John and Jesus.

- Finish the Jesse Tree. Add Elizabeth and Zechariah near John the Baptist. Add the figures of Mary and Jesus at the top. In Christian tradition, Mary is represented by both the Madonna lily and the Rose, so you could add either or both near to her figure. Make a star to add to the top on Christmas Day.

- Although a small place, Bethlehem was a town of significance to the Jewish people. Use Bible dictionaries to discover some of the things which happened at Bethlehem during the Old Testament period.

- The traditional themes of Advent are of preparation, concern for others and spiritual readiness. The Mexican custom of the *Posada* helps the congregation to focus on these themes. Dress up one child as Mary and another as Joseph (and also include the donkey if you can find the costume!). Go around the parish singing carols. At the homes of chosen parishioners get 'Mary' and 'Joseph' to knock on the door and ask for a room for the night. The parishioners need to act as belligerent innkeepers who reject the group. The group finally arrives at the church where the congregation warmly welcomes them. There can then be a short service or Blessing of the Crib.

A more detailed explanation of the *Posada* can be found in *Seasons, Saints and Sticky Tape*.

Prayers/ intercessions

God and Father of our coming Lord Jesus Christ, the time of Christ's advent draws near and we feel a mixture of excitement and apprehension. Excitement for the hope he heralds; apprehension for the judgement he brings. This yearly round brings pain as well as pleasure.

We are innkeepers, for our hearts are too ready to cry: 'No room here!' and yet we want to be the shepherds who heard the angels, and gathered in wonder and praise at the cradle:

Leader   Lord, come to the help of your servants.

All   **Remember your promise of mercy.**

We are Herods, fearful for our position, and yet we want to be the wise men who bowed and gave gifts.

Leader   Lord, come to the help of your servants.

All   **Remember your promise of mercy.**

We ache to welcome the Christ–child, and yet we agonize at the cost of commitment.

Leader   Lord, come to the help of your servants.

All   **Remember your promise of mercy.**

Living God, fill us with wonder and keen anticipation for the glory to be revealed. Take from us unfitting fear and give us an expectation of renewal. Speak to us of your enduring nearness as we draw near to you in worship.

Leader   Lord, come to the help of your servants.

All   **Remember your promise of mercy.**

           Maranatha. Come, Lord Jesus.

Stephen Brown, 'God and Father of our coming Lord', in Donald Hilton (ed.), *Seasons and Celebrations*

Stories and other resources

John and Janet Perkins, *Haffertee's First Christmas*, Lion, 1977

Paddie Devon, *The Grumpy Shepherd*, Scripture Union, 1995

Papa Panov's Special Day, Lion, 1988

Selina Hastings (ed.), 'The birth of John', in *The Illustrated Children's Bible,* Dorling Kindersley, 1994

Donald Hilton (ed.), *Seasons and Celebrations*, NCEC, 1996

Katie Thompson, 'Blessed are you' (Fourth Sunday of Advent Year C), in *The Complete Children's Liturgy Book*, Kevin Mayhew, 1995

The Advent section, in *Seasons, Saints and Sticky Tape* (p. 5)

 # Drama

Derek Haylock, 'Guardian angels', in *Acts for Apostles,* NS/CHP, 1987

 # Music

Come, Lord Jesus, come (BBP 29 and JU p. 88) – verses 1, 2, 3 and 4 this week

The virgin Mary had a baby boy (JP 251)

Who came to Mary? (BBP 30)

From heaven you came (SHF 120)

When he comes (SHF 599)

He came down (JU p. 36)

He was born a little child (Malawi song – WP 28)

O come, O come, Emmanuel (HAMNS 26, HON 358, HTC 66)

Tell out, my soul (HAMNS 422, HON 467, HTC 42, SHF 498)

Post communion prayer

Heavenly Father,
who chose the Blessed Virgin Mary
to be the mother of the promised saviour:
fill us your servants with your grace,
that in all things we may embrace your holy will
and with her rejoice in your salvation;
through Jesus Christ our Lord.

Christmas Day

25 December

Readings (Set III)

Isaiah 52.7-10

This prophecy foretells the time when the messenger will bring good news that will proclaim peace, good tidings and salvation. Even the 'ruins of Jerusalem' will burst into songs of joy at the coming of the salvation of God to all the ends of the earth.

Hebrews 1.1-4[5-12]

God's message was spoken to the people of the past through the prophets. Now, in these last days, it is through Jesus that God's message can be heard.

John 1.1-14

Jesus is the Word become flesh. Through him all things were made and his life is the light to all people. Although many do not recognise him, he gives the right to become children of God to all who would receive him.

Alternatively, the following sets of readings may be used:

I.	Isaiah 9.2-7	II.	Isaiah 62.6-12
	Titus 2.11-14		Titus 3.4-7
	Luke 2.1-14 [15-20]		Luke 2.[1-7]8-20

Collect

Almighty God,
you have given us your only-begotten Son
to take our nature upon him
and as at this time to be born of a pure virgin:
grant that we, who have been born again
and made your children by adoption and grace,
may daily be renewed by your Holy Spirit;
through Jesus Christ your Son our Lord,
who is alive and reigns with you,
in the unity of the Holy Spirit,
one God, now and for ever.

Talk/address/ sermon

There are many ways of explaining the good news of Jesus' birth and its significance for us today. The following visual aids are a useful starting point for the Christmas talk.

- The crib

Gather the younger children around the crib. Talk about each of the figures and the part they play in the Christmas story. Choose children to add the baby Jesus and additional angels, shepherds, etc to the crib scene.

- The Advent wreath

Explain the symbolism of the wreath – with the central ring representing the world, the purple candles our longing for God's forgiveness and the pink candle our joy in awaiting the arrival of the Saviour. Light the central white candle and discuss the ways that Jesus brings light into our world.

- The visitors

Choose members of the congregation and dress them as the shepherds. Tell the story of the visit of the shepherds to see Jesus, using the verses from Luke 2.8-20 or using your own words. Ask the chosen 'shepherds' to act out the story.

What would it have been like to have witnessed all that they did? What did they learn about Jesus from their experience?

- 'The whole picture'

Use the pictures, produced earlier in the groups, to re-tell the nativity story.

Congregational/ group activities

- Enact the Christmas story, using both adults and children for the narration and acting. Often the best nativity plays are written and planned by church members. However, there are a number of simple but effective versions available. *Children Aloud!* has two such Nativity plays.

- Give each member of the congregation a piece of paper or card. Discuss how Christmas is not only a time for giving to our family, but of thinking of others in need. Ask each person to write a short prayer (or draw a picture) about a person/nation that is particularly in need of God's love and care. All these prayers can be collected up in a large box, decorated like a present, and placed next to the crib.

- Give each group a large sheet of paper (A1 size if possible) and part of the Christmas story that they must illustrate. (It would be worth working out in advance how many groups you might have and dividing the story into a corresponding number of sections – such as the angel's visit to Mary, the journey to Bethlehem, the visit of the shepherds, etc.) Use these as visual aids during the talk, or to decorate the church.

- Ask people in advance to bring in their favourite Christmas cards. What do the people like about them and why are they special? What kind of message do they give about Christmas?

Prayers/ intercessions

Use the responsive intercessions for Christmas from *Patterns for Worship* on pages 66–9.

Alternatively, use the prayers and pictures that were produced earlier in the groups.

Stories and other resources

Paddie Devon, *The Grumpy Shepherd*, Scripture Union, 1995

Sheila Forsdyke, 'The girl who saw Christmas', in *Together for Festivals*, NS/CHP, 1997

Kenneth Steven, 'The night before Christmas', in *Together for Festivals*, NS/CHP, 1997

Gordon and Ronni Lamont, *Children Aloud!*, NS/CHP, 1997

Betty Pedley, 'Jesus' birthday party', in *Together with Children*, Nov/Dec 1996

The Incarnation section in *Pick and Mix* (p. 93). The Christmas sections, in *Festive Allsort*s (p. 8), *Seasons, Saints and Sticky Tape* (p. 12) and *Building New Bridges* (p. 52).

Drama

Paul Burbridge and Murray Watts, 'The two shepherds', in *The Best Time to Act*, Hodder & Stoughton, 1995

Michael Forster, 'No room', in *Act One*, Kevin Mayhew, 1996

Derek Haylock, 'We can't see Jesus!/I wonder what happened to him?', in *Plays for All Seasons*, NS/CHP, 1997

Ruth Tiller, 'Come and worship/The shepherd king/We have to go to Bethlehem', in *Keeping the Feast*, Kevin Mayhew, 1995

Dave Hopwood, 'Silent night', in *Fistful of Sketches*, NS/CHP, 1996

Music

All the traditional carols are obviously appropriate for today's service.

Joy to the world! (HON 283, HTC 197)

Lord Jesus Christ (HAMNS 391, HON 311, HTC 417)

Thou didst leave thy throne (HAMNS 250, HON 513)

Unto us a boy is born! (HON 526)

A baby was born in Bethlehem (WP 1)

In a stable (WP 35)

How lovely on the mountains (HON 219, SHF 176)

Go, tell it on the mountain (HON 165)

See him lying on a bed of straw (Calypso carol – HON 440)

Post communion prayer

God our Father,
whose Word has come among us
in the Holy Child of Bethlehem:
may the light of faith illumine our hearts
    and shine in our words and deeds;
through him who is Christ the Lord.

The First Sunday of Christmas

 ## Readings

1 Samuel 2.18-20,26

Samuel was born to his mother Hannah as a gift of God after years of humiliating childlessness and, in consequence, she consecrated him in God's service in the Temple as a small child. Here we read of Samuel's parents visiting their child as he served God under the care of Eli, the priest, and that as well as growing physically, he grew in closeness to God and to other people.

Colossians 3.12-17

The writer describes what should be the characteristics of those who follow Christ, and how they should show their response to God. Love will hold them together and they will show Christ's peace in the way they behave.

Luke 2.41-52

This is the only Bible story we have of Jesus' childhood. At twelve Jesus is old enough to participate in the adult customs of the Jewish faith, and the journey to Jerusalem indicates that he was a member of a devout family. The incident in the Temple emphasizes again that he is no ordinary child; the whole story is leading up to his statement that he is in his 'Father's house'. The puzzlement of his parents at this underlines how extraordinary Jesus is to be.

Collect

Almighty God,
who wonderfully created us in your own image
and yet more wonderfully restored us
through your Son Jesus Christ:
grant that, as he came to share in our humanity,
so we may share the life of his divinity;
who is alive and reigns with you,
in the unity of the Holy Spirit,
one God, now and for ever.

 ## Talk/address/ sermon

Luke is the only Gospel writer to provide any account of any incident in Jesus' childhood and, like his birth narrative, it links and yet contrasts the naturally human and the extraordinary nature of Jesus. It puzzled his parents and it puzzles us.

The reading may seem an odd choice for the Sunday after Christmas: the passing of twelve years is marked in less than a week. But it challenges the temptation to sentimentality which is the danger of the nativity story: the weakness and vulnerability of the child in the manger is contrasted with the boy who can challenge even the most knowledgeable teachers in the foremost seat of learning of his nation.

 ## Congregational/ group activities

- Light all five candles on the Advent (now Christmas) Wreath and share experiences of Christmas. You might note down one experience of each member to use in thanksgiving prayer.

- Find out about the celebration of bar mitzvah, the ceremony which marks the time when Jewish boys today take on the adult responsibilities of their faith.

- Play hide and seek. Talk about looking for things that are lost. What does it feel like to have lost something? And how do you feel when you find it again? What experiences do you have of being lost and how did you feel? Discuss this and then role-play the Gospel story unpacking the emotions involved. Sum this up by singing 'Once in Royal David's City' together.

- In the Colossians passage we read of singing 'psalms, hymns and spiritual songs' with gratitude. Invite everyone to decide which is their favourite Christmas carol and to work out why they like it, then to share this with other people in a group or with the whole congregation.

Prayers/ intercessions

Give thanks for all the joys of Christmas time:
the gift of Jesus to the world as a baby;
the gift of light to a dark world;
the joy of worship and singing carols;
the joy of celebration and the fun of parties;
the love of families and the joy of being together.

'Glory to God', a Peruvian traditional song, might be used as a simple sung response to these biddings, a singer leading the congregation in response. The 'Alleluia, Amen' may be kept for the end of the prayers (JU p. 78).

Stories and other resources

Selina Hastings (ed.), 'Jesus is found in the Temple', in *The Children's Illustrated Bible*, Dorling Kindersley, 1994

Pat Alexander, 'Jesus grows up', in *The Young Puffin Book of Bible Stories*, Puffin, 1988

Leslie Francis and Nicola Slee, *Lights: Teddy Horsley Celebrates Christmas,* NCEC, 1985

The Christmas section, in *Seasons, Saints and Sticky Tape* (p. 12) and *Festive Allsorts* (p. 18)

 ## Drama

Dave Hopwood, 'Silent night', in *A Fistful of Sketches*, NS/CHP, 1996

Music

It is usual to continue to sing Christmas carols on this Sunday. 'Once in Royal David's City' is particularly appropriate to the Gospel reading. The following songs are also suitable for this Sunday:

The King is among us (HON 483, SHF 511)

Glory to God (Peruvian Gloria – HON 161, BBP 49, JU p. 78)

Come on and celebrate! (HON 95, SHF 69)

You are the King who reigns (SHF 631)

Christ was born in Bethlehem (BBP 36)

A baby was born in Bethlehem (WP 1)

Post communion prayer

Heavenly Father,
whose blessed Son shared at Nazareth
    the life of an earthly home:
help your Church to live as one family,
united in love and obedience,
and bring us all at last to our home in heaven;
through Jesus Christ our Lord.

The Second Sunday of Christmas

 ## Readings

Jeremiah 31.7-14

Many commentators suggest that this passage represents the high point of prophetic writing. The prophet writes of the restoration of Israel, the saving of God's people. Even the sick and the frail, and those scattered far away will return to a land of plenty, where they will be comforted and they will respond with rejoicing.

or

Ecclesiasticus 24.1-12

Wisdom tells of her relationship with God from the beginning and how she has taken root in God's chosen people. The passage mirrors the Gospel reading, with its allusion to God's work both in the past and in the present – his presence in creation and also with his present–day followers.

Ephesians 1.3-14

This great blessing matches the Gospel reading in the intensity of its emotion. God is blessed for the gift of Christ and we are made God's people through him. The writing echoes the Old Testament notion of God's chosen people.

John 1.[1-9]10-18

In this beautiful poem John, the Gospel writer, describes Christ as the creator who comes to his people, only to be rejected by them. He comes to reveal God's glory, for those who choose to see it. The poem reminds the reader of the witness to Jesus of John the Baptist, which we encountered in the Advent readings, and now reveals that Jesus Christ is the one who came to make God known.

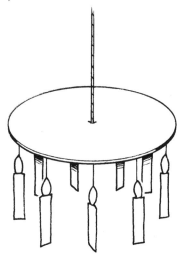

Collect

Almighty God,
in the birth of your Son
you have poured on us the new light of your
   incarnate Word,
and shown us the fullness of your love:
help us to walk in his light and dwell in his love
that we may know the fullness of his joy;
who is alive and reigns with you,
in the unity of the Holy Spirit,
one God, now and for ever.

 ## Talk/address/ sermon

Use a calendar as a visual aid in your address/sermon.

As a new calendar year begins we also celebrate God's new beginning. The Incarnation, the coming of Jesus, marks the new covenant, a new relationship between God and his people.

Discuss the type of New Year resolutions that we make.

At this time we often make New Year resolutions, in an effort to start afresh. What New Year resolutions can we make about our faith? How will we show the difference that our faith makes?

 ## Congregational/ group activities

* Make a mobile which reflects today's Gospel reading using verses 12-20 from Psalm 147. A simple way to do this would be to cut out a large circle from card. Give each person a candle template to

draw around and to cut out the shape of the candle. Decorate these candles with gold foil. Attach each of these candles to the circle of card with fine thread.

Decorate the main circle of card with the pictures suggested by verses 12-20 of the psalm and write the words: 'The light shines in the darkness, and the darkness did not overcome it.' Concentrate particularly on the descriptions of creation; depict people of all ages praising God.

- Explain carefully what will happen during this activity in advance. Turn out the lights in the church and ensure it is as dark as possible. Talk about the feeling of being in darkness and try to imagine occasions in everyday life when people feel like that. Light a candle and talk about the difference this makes to people's feelings. Make a collage which shows the light which Christ brings to a dark world. Include words from the Gospel reading in it and also these words: 'A small candle can destroy the darkness but the darkness can never destroy the light of a small candle.'

- Perform the drama 'Light of the World' from *Plays on the Word* (Derek Haylock, NS/CHP, 1993).

- This would be a good day to use Christingles in a service if you do not use them on another occasion in your church.

- Read together the passages from John's Gospel and from Ephesians. On a large sheet of paper write the words of John 1.12 and Ephesians 1.3. Then list ways in which the coming of Jesus has helped humanity to understand better what God is like and what God wants of us, his people. Use the sheets as the basis for thanksgiving and prayer.

Prayers/ intercessions

Give thanks for the mystery of creation; for God's gift in making himself known through Jesus; for the freedom which Christ came to bring. Use this response:

Leader Blessed be God, the Father of our Lord Jesus Christ

All **who has blessed us in Christ.**

Pray that we may be effective witnesses of the gospel; pray for those who do not know God's grace; pray for those who suffer and need the support of our prayers and our lives.

Use this response:

Leader May the light of Christ shine through us for others

All **now and for ever.**

Stories and other resources

Chapters 8 and 9 of *The Magician's Nephew* by C. S. Lewis describe the birth of Narnia. The section which begins, 'This is an empty world. This is nothing.' provides a way in for children and others to today's Gospel reading.

Leslie Francis and Nicola Slee, *Lights: Teddy Horsley Celebrates Christmas*, NCEC, 1985

Katie Thompson, 'God sends his son, Jesus' (Second Sunday after Christmas, Year C), in *The Complete Children's Liturgy Book*, Kevin Mayhew, 1995

'Incarnation', in *Pick and Mix* (p. 93)

Drama

Derek Haylock, 'Light of the world', in *Plays on the Word*, NS/CHP, 1993

Music

Adoramus te, Domine (MT1 p. 42, HON 7)

From the darkness came light (CP1 29)

Come, Lord Jesus, come (BBP 29, JU p. 88) – particularly verse 5 this week

He made the stars to shine (JU p. 70)

A special star (BBP 37)

Lord, the light of your love is shining (HON 317)

Of the Father's heart begotten (HAMNS 33, HTC 56)

Christ is the world's true light (HAMNS 346, HON 78)

As with gladness men of old (HAMNS 51, HON 41, HTC 99)

Post communion prayer

All praise to you,
almighty God and heavenly King,
who sent your Son into the world
to take our nature upon him
and to be born of a pure virgin:
grant that, as we are born again in him,
so he may continually dwell in us
and reign on earth as he reigns in heaven,
now and for ever.

Epiphany

January 6th

In any year when there is a Second Sunday of Christmas, the Epiphany may also be celebrated on this Sunday.

As the readings are the same for Years A and C, please refer to the other books in the *Worship through the Christian Year* series for further ideas.

 ### Readings

Isaiah 60:1-6

The prophet foretells a time when, out of the darkness that covers the earth, will come a light that will draw nations and kings to it.

Ephesians 3:1-12

Paul, writing from prison, tells how the mystery of Christ has been revealed to the Gentiles. The gospel of Christ has broken the boundaries between Israel and the Gentiles, who are now members together of one body and sharers together in the promises in Christ Jesus.

Matthew 2.1-12

The Magi, or wise men, come to Jerusalem in search of the one born to be King of the Jews, following the star that will guide them to him. King Herod is disturbed by their message and discovers, from his chief priests and teachers of the law, that the Christ is to be born in Bethlehem. He sends the wise men there to find the child. They find Jesus and worship him, giving him the gifts of gold, frankincense and myrrh.

Collect

> O God,
> who by the leading of a star
> manifested your only Son to the peoples of the
>   earth:
> mercifully grant that we,
> who know you now by faith,
> may at last behold your glory face to face;
> through Jesus Christ your Son our Lord,
> who is alive and reigns with you,
> in the unity of the Holy Spirit,
> one God, now and for ever.

 ### Talk/address/ sermon

Take in one or two of your favourite Christmas presents. Explain why these are important and special to you.

What were your favourite Christmas presents? Why are they special to you?

What was so special about the wise men's gifts and what was their significance to Jesus? What is their significance to us today?

The book *Festive Allsorts* provides a useful summary of the symbolism of the three gifts.

 ### Congregational/ group activities

- Re-enact the story of the wise men's visit to Jesus. Either use adults and children to act out the story during the Bible reading, or repeat this segment of the Christmas story from the nativity play that the children performed several weeks earlier.

- Give out a cardboard star for each member of the congregation. Ask them to write on each point of the star one of the following words: Church, world, local community, sick, bereaved. Then ask them to write or draw a picture of one item to pray for in each of these areas.

- Hold an Epiphany party, using ideas such as cut-out party crowns, star-shaped biscuits and sweets wrapped in wrapping paper as 'gifts' for the children.

- Make a small 'theatre' from a cardboard box, with different backdrops for the scenes in the story. Draw the figures in the story on thin card and cut out and mount these cards on 'pea sticks', so they can be added from the two sides of the theatre. A detailed description of this activity is given in the Epiphany section of *Seasons, Saints and Sticky Tape*.

- Discuss the following questions in groups: Can you remember any of the gifts you were given last Christmas? What is the most precious gift you have been given and why? What are the usual presents that are given to a new-born baby? Why did the wise men bring the gifts of gold, frankincense and myrrh to Jesus?

Prayers/ intercessions

Pray in turn for the following five topics: Church, world, local community, sick, bereaved. Pause at the end of each prayer, allowing time for the congregation to quietly pray for the points they wrote on their prayer stars.

Alternatively, ask the congregation to pray in their groups, using the prayers that they wrote on their prayer stars.

Use the response:

Leader The light of Christ, that has entered the world

All **lighten our darkness and bring us your peace.**

Stories and other resources

Phyllis Jackson, 'The adventure of three mice', in *Together for Festivals*, NS/CHP, 1997

Jenny Loxston, 'The star: an Epiphany all–age service', in *Together for Festivals*, NS/CHP, 1997

Betty Pedley and John Muir, 'All–age service for Epiphany', in *Children in the Church?*, NS/CHP, 1997

The Epiphany sections, in *Pick and Mix* and *Seasons, Saints and Sticky Tape*

Drama

Michael Forster, 'Ride that camel! Follow that star!', in *Act One*, Kevin Mayhew, 1996

Gordon and Ronni Lamont, 'The tale of the Wise Ones', in *Children Aloud!*, NS/CHP, 1997

Sue Hardgrave, 'Gifts for the giver', in *Together for Festivals*, NS/CHP, 1997

Dave Hopwood, 'The wisdom of the wise', in *A Fistful of Sketches*, NS/CHP, 1996

Michael Forster, 'A camel's eye view', *Act Two*, Kevin Mayhew, 1996

Music

As with gladness men of old (HAMNS 51, HON 41, HTC 99)

Christ is the world's true light (HAMNS 346, HON 78)

We three kings of Orient are (HON 537)

Come on and celebrate! (HON 95, SHF 69)

The Lord is my light (HON 486)

The light of Christ (MP 652)

This little light of mine (JP 258)

Kindle a flame to lighten the dark (WGS1 p. 135)

Post communion prayer

Lord God,
the bright splendour whom the nations seek:
may we who with the wise men
    have been drawn by your light
discern the glory of your presence in your Son,
the Word made flesh, Jesus Christ our Lord.

The Baptism of Christ

The First Sunday of Epiphany

 ## Readings

Isaiah 43.1-7

This is a poem of huge power using very clever imagery to develop its message. God is in control of the waters, both literal – recalling the escape from Egypt – and metaphorical – in terms of troubles or trials. God is seen to be a special God, prepared to make great sacrifices for his people whom he greatly loves. The section closes with an image of the gathering together of all God's people from the very ends of the earth.

Acts 8.14-17

This story, apparently simple but showing a very clear understanding of the idea of the Trinity, describes how the apostles send Peter and John to pray with the believers in Samaria so that they may receive the Holy Spirit. The reading links closely with today's Gospel reading and clearly shows the importance of the disciples' work as representing the whole of the Godhead.

Luke 3.15,17,21-22

The completeness of Jesus' baptism is graphically shown in the second part of the reading; the Son, the Spirit and the Father all together as man, dove and voice. There are tremendous echoes of the creation where God's voice is heard bringing the world into being. When taken with the first part of the reading it can be seen that this creation has reached some kind of fulfilment, as the Son being addressed is none other than the long-awaited Messiah.

Collect

> Eternal Father,
> who at the baptism of Jesus
> revealed him to be your Son,
> anointing him with the Holy Spirit:
> grant to us, who are born again by water and the
>   Spirit,
> that we may be faithful to our calling
>   as your adopted children;
> through Jesus Christ your Son our Lord,
> who is alive and reigns with you,
> in the unity of the Holy Spirit,
> one God, now and for ever.

 ## Talk/address/ sermon

Bring in a baptism candle and certificate (your own if you can) to introduce the talk. This event in Jesus' life is crucial. It is his outward expression of obedience to God, and God's corresponding recognition of Jesus as his Son, at the beginning of his ministry. This is the first time that Jesus appears as an adult, yet we have only just celebrated his birth! This aspect of the Church year needs careful handling. It provides an opportunity to explore the contrast between the **narrative** and **symbolic** aspects of the Church year.

When was your baptism? What was it the beginning of? Who was at your baptism?

Who was at Jesus' baptism?

 ## Congregational/ group activities

- Make 'kinetic' (or moving) displays to depict the baptism of Jesus. Draw an outline of a figure on a thin piece of card. Cut a line from A to B. Attach a dove/bird shape C to card strip D through incision E–F. The dove can then be moved up and down A–B to symbolize the Holy Spirit descending.

- Share names in pairs or small groups, of mixed age, and if possible the meaning of those names. Encourage older and younger people in the congregation to write their names onto cards and then pin them up – it is unlikely that even within the church everyone knows each other's names.

- Re-affirmation of our own baptism.

   This would not be a re-enactment, but a chance to think again about what baptism means to us. This could be simply done by saying together the baptismal responses or the Nicene creed. A more complex approach might involve the use of the baptismal candles or saying prayers of dedication. (An example of these can be found in *Emmaus: The Way of Faith, Nurture Book*, NS/CHP, 1996, p. 79.)

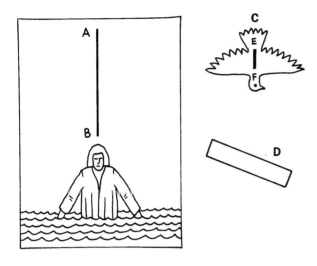

Send us out in his power
to live and work to your praise and glory;
through him to whom we belong,
Jesus Christ our Lord. Amen.

Galatians 5.22, 23
Church Family Worship (no. 324)

Stories and other resources

'The Renewal of Baptismal Vows', in *The Alternative Service Book* (p. 275), Clowes/SPCK/Cambridge University Press, 1980

Leslie Francis and Nicola Slee, *Water: Teddy Horsley and Baptism*, NCEC, 1996

Patterns for Worship (pp. 75–7,116,159,183)

'Baptism', in *Pick and Mix* (p. 15)

Music

God's love (JU p. 90)

Such love (SHF 490)

The steadfast love of the Lord (SHF 541)

Cleanse me from my sin (JP 27)

I'm special (JP 106)

It's hard to say 'I'm sorry' (BBP 75)

Be thou my vision (HAMNS 343, HON 56, HTC 545, SHF 38)

When Jesus came to Jordan (HAMNS 526)

Hail to the Lord's anointed (HAMNS 142, HON 193, HTC 190, SHF 146)

Prayers/intercessions

Have a time of thanksgiving to God:

* for his power over all of creation, yet he is with us, his chosen ones;
* to celebrate the gift of the Holy Spirit to all of us in our baptism;
* for God's closeness to his people.

Use the response:

Leader   Lord, come to bless us:

All   **and fill us with your Spirit.**

Use prayers appropriate for a baptism service, such as those from *Patterns for Worship* on pages 75–7 and 116.

Use the following responses at the end of the service:

'The fruit of the Spirit is love, joy and peace.'
Father, we know that your world needs love and
  harmony: come to bless us,
and fill us with your Spirit.

'The fruit of the Spirit is patience, kindness and
  goodness.'
Father, we know that our world is starved of
  compassion and true fellowship: come to bless us,
and fill us with your Spirit.

'The fruit of the Spirit is faithfulness, gentleness
  and self–control.'
Father, we know that our world is short of truth and
  justice: come to bless us,
and fill us with your Spirit.

Post communion prayer

Lord of all time and eternity,
  you opened the heavens
    and revealed yourself as Father
in the baptism of Jesus your beloved Son:
by the power of your Spirit
complete the heavenly work of our rebirth
through the waters of the new creation;
through Jesus Christ our Lord.

The Second Sunday of Epiphany

 ## Readings

Isaiah 62.1-5

This passage uses the striking imagery of marriage to depict the relationship between God and Jerusalem. The intensity of feeling felt by the bridegroom for the bride is such as is felt by God for Jerusalem, and by implication for the world.

1 Corinthians 12.1-11

Paul begins this passage by showing how it is by the Holy Spirit that we recognize Christ's lordship. Paul then goes on to identify some precise consequences of receiving the Spirit of God in terms of the gifts that are given to the people of God.

John 2.1-11

The wedding at Cana is the setting for Jesus' first miracle. Jesus is reluctant to respond to the need of the wedding party but does so after the intervention of his mother. This act of changing water into wine can be seen as a response from Jesus to the needs of those around him. It is a clear revelation (or epiphany!) of the power of Christ. The significance of this miracle lies in the quiet assumption of Jesus' power. There is no 'miracle-working', no ostentatious demonstration of power. Christ's authority over creation is simply stated in the act of Jesus himself and is simply reported by John.

Collect

Almighty God,
in Christ you make all things new:
transform the poverty of our nature
    by the riches of your grace,
and in the renewal of our lives
make known your heavenly glory;
through Jesus Christ your Son our Lord,
who is alive and reigns with you,
in the unity of the Holy Spirit,
one God, now and for ever.

 ## Talk/address/ sermon

Before the service prepare a box full of wrapped-up presents. Invite children to open the box and then open the gifts inside. Each one might contain a small gift for the child (such as a sweet) along with a sheet of paper with one of the gifts of the Spirit written on it. This serves as an illustration of God's goodness in giving to each of us. Gifts are, of course, dependent on the giver. This is rather striking these days when children are encouraged to ask for (or are asked about) the gifts they receive. God's gifts, unlike these, are often surprises!

When do we receive gifts or presents? How did you feel when opening these presents? What did you expect to find inside? What gifts does God give to each of us (such as the gifts of sight and hearing)? Do we take these gifts for granted?

Congregational/ group activities

- Collect together some wedding photos. It would be nice to get ones from families within the local community but if you cannot do this then there are often wedding photos published in local papers that you can use. Or you could buy a copy of something like *Brides* magazine. Look at the pictures and talk about the feelings of the brides and grooms. How might these feelings be felt by God?

- Create a 'gift' collage depicting the gifts of the Spirit. Cut out illustrations from magazines that symbolize the gifts. It is possible to find illustrations of many of the gifts (such as love), though some of them, such as faith, might be difficult. The advantage of this activity is that you will be able to see where children need help in understanding the different gifts. You might also discover that children will be able to explain why their picture illustrates faith or one of the other gifts.

- God has given to us; what can we give to God? Before the offertory invite the congregation of all ages to write or draw onto paper things that they could give to God. During the offertory have these papers gathered in so that they are made part of the congregation's offering to God along with the money.

- Write a thank-you letter to God from the church. Using an OHP, have a standard letter ready but invite different members of the congregation to contribute suggestions of gifts from God that we might like to say 'thank-you' for.

 ## Prayers/ intercessions

Offer prayers of thanksgiving:

- for the wholeness that comes with the communion with God;

- for we who are the Church, that we might receive and share the gifts of the Spirit.

Use the 'gifts' identified in the Activities section. Emphasize the specific ways your church has benefited. Use the following response:

Leader   For all your gifts to us:

All   **we thank you, gracious God.**

 ## Stories and other resources

Susan Sayers, 'Accepting God's gift', in *More Things to Do in Children's Worship*, Kevin Mayhew, 1996

Patterns for Worship (pp. 75–7,159)

'Gifts', in *Pick and Mix* (p. 68)

 ## Music

Be still and know (SHF 37)

Let us consecrate our lives (SHF 322)

Shalom (CP2 141)

Peace is flowing like a river (HON 412, SHF 431)

Heav'n shall not wait (HON 207)

Father of heav'n, whose love profound (HAMNS 97, HON 124, HTC 359)

Lord Jesus Christ (HAMNS 391, HON 311, HTC 417, SHF 342)

Come, Holy Spirit, come! (HON 93)

Post communion prayer

God of glory,
you nourish us with your Word
who is the bread of life:
fill us with your Holy Spirit
that through us the light of your glory
may shine in all the world.
We ask this in the name of Jesus Christ our Lord.

The Third Sunday of Epiphany

 ## Readings

Nehemiah 8.1-3,5-6,8-10

The reading of the Law is an integral part of the life of the Jew. Each year at the beginning and the completion of the reading of the Law there is a festival, the Simchat Torah.

In this reading we see Ezra telling the people to go and celebrate, to go and feast. This is because the Law is a cause for feasting and celebration. It is God's Law and as such leads us to celebrate God's creation of us, God's saving of us and God's gifts to us. We see in this reading a prefiguring of the goodness of God that is to come to the world.

1 Corinthians 12.12-31a

Paul compares the variety and unity of the gifts of the Spirit with the human anatomy. He demonstrates that all the parts of the body are essential to the well-being of the body as a whole. Each individual, whatever gift they have received from God, has a vital part to play in the life and unity of the Church.

Luke 4.14-21

Jesus uses the words of Isaiah to proclaim his message of good news. This passage, perhaps above all, provides the vital link between the Old and the New Testaments. Jesus speaks of the Spirit of the Lord as a galvanizing force, as a sign of chosenness. Again, the coming of Jesus is shown as the fulfilment of the Old Testament. The striking political message of verses 16-17 cannot be dodged; it is particularly to the poor, the captives, the oppressed, the blind, that Jesus brings the message of good news.

Collect

Almighty God,
whose Son revealed in signs and miracles
the wonder of your saving presence:
renew your people with your heavenly grace,
and in all our weakness
sustain us by your mighty power;
through Jesus Christ your Son our Lord,
who is alive and reigns with you,
in the unity of the Holy Spirit,
one God, now and for ever.

 ## Talk/address/ sermon

Draw a picture of the human body. Cut this into pieces and hide the parts around the church before the service begins. At the beginning of the talk, choose three or four children to find the pieces. Assemble the parts and discuss the importance of each one. Lead into talking about Paul's use of the body as an illustration for the Church.

Alternatively, use the following questions to discuss the mission of the Church.

How are the mission of the Church and the mission of Christ related? In what ways do we as the Church bring good news to the poor, liberate captives, bring sight to the blind, free the oppressed? How do we as the Church 'proclaim the year of the Lord's favour'? Do we do this at all? Do we make this a bargain – come to church and God will save you? Do we, like Christ, go out with the good news to those very people mentioned in verse 16?

 ## Congregational/ group activities

- Paul uses the body as an example of what we can all give. Design two large pictures in the groups; the first showing different body parts and the need for all of them; the second showing a group of people who are needed by us all. Identify those who do vital work despite being outside the 'Church' as such.

- Discuss how the 'Law of God' can be a gift. How do we see the Law of God? Is this just another set of rules? What are the rules that we know? This would be a good opportunity to look at the ten commandments as they really are, not just as a set of moral precepts. Focus particularly on the first three about God.

- 'What am I?' activity. Each member of the congregation is asked to write or draw what part of the body they think they are most like (using Paul's analogy from the Corinthians reading). Draw a large outline of the human body and stick people's sheets of paper in the appropriate places. Ask people to come forward and tell, briefly, why they feel that they might be a particular body part.

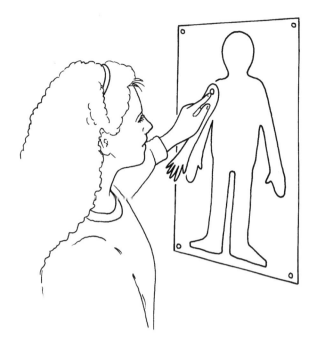

- Choose a volunteer and draw around their body. Write in the parts of the body. What part would each of the people see themselves as being?

Prayers/ intercessions

Give thanks to God:

- for God's Law;

- for the reasons to celebrate that God has given us: for the world, for Jesus, for the gift of the Holy Spirit.

Pray that we may all use our own gifts to be a benefit to the whole body of Christ. Ask for God's strength in our own mission. As the body of Christ we follow in Jesus' footsteps; we need the Spirit just as he did.

Focus on hands and how these can be used for both good and bad purposes. Use the prayer suggestion from 'When you pray', Worksheet 13 in *Children and Holy Communion*. This uses the fingers of the hand to remind us of different things to pray for:

- **thumb**: this is the **strongest** finger. Pray for all the strong things in your life, like home and family, that protect and take care of you.

- **index finger**: the **pointing** finger. Pray for all those who guide and help, like teachers, clergy, doctors, fire and police services.

- **middle finger**: this is the **tallest** finger. Pray for all those who have power in the world.

- **ring finger**: this is the **weakest** finger. It cannot do much by itself. Pray for the poor, weak and helpless.

- **little finger**: the **smallest** and **last** finger. Pray for yourself.

Stories and other resources

Leslie Francis and Nicola Slee, *Neighbours*, NCEC, 1990

Anita Haigh, 'March for justice' (a chant), in *Rap, Rhyme and Reason*, Scripture Union, 1996

The sections on the Missionary and Caring Church, in *Church Family Worship* (nos. 413–461)

Patterns for Worship (pp. 80–81)

The sections on 'Hands and feet', in *Under Fives – Alive!* (p. 29) and *Praise, Play and Paint* (p. 101)

 ## Music

I am the church (JU p. 24, BBP 48)

The body song (JU p. 62)

Playing, running, skipping, jumping (JU p. 32, BBP 23)

For I'm building a people of power (SHF 109)

He's got the whole world (JU p. 60)

Two little eyes (JU p. 58)

God's Spirit is in my heart (HON 180)

All praise to thee, for thou, O King divine (HAMNS 337, HON 18)

God is working his purpose out (HON 172, HTC 188)

Hark the glad sound! (HAMNS 30, HON 198, HTC 193)

Post communion prayer

Almighty Father,
whose Son our Saviour Jesus Christ
   is the light of the world:
may your people,
illumined by your word and sacraments,
shine with the radiance of his glory,
that he may be known, worshipped, and obeyed
   to the ends of the earth;
for he is alive and reigns, now and for ever.

The Fourth Sunday of Epiphany

 ## Readings

Ezekiel 43.27 – 44.4

The Lord continues to give instructions on how the priests and Levites are to use his Temple. They are commanded to keep the outer gate of the sanctuary shut, as the Lord himself has entered through it: only the prince is allowed to sit inside the gateway to eat in the presence of the Lord.

1 Corinthians 13.1-13

Paul's great exposition on the virtues of love is one of the best-known passages in the Bible. It is a continuation of Paul's reply to the issues raised by the Corinthians. He is trying to draw them out from a narrow response to following God into a 'life–wide' involvement in the kingdom. Again there is a striving for a complete understanding – what we see now is only partial, yet in all this partiality there remains love.

Luke 2.22-40

In the first part of the reading we retrace Jesus' boyhood and the presentation in the Temple, together with the responses of Simeon and Anna. Simeon's response is familiarly known as the Nunc Dimittis. Its first line ('Sovereign Lord, as you have promised, you now dismiss your servant in peace') refers to both a personal promise to Simeon and a public promise made throughout the history of Israel that God would bring about their salvation.

The second part of the reading is much shorter but is significant in commenting on how Jesus grew and was 'filled with wisdom, and the favour of God was upon him'. By the time he visits the Temple in the next passage he is already twelve years old!

Collect

God our creator,
who in the beginning
commanded the light to shine out of darkness:
we pray that the light of the glorious gospel of Christ
may dispel the darkness of ignorance and un-belief,
shine into the hearts of all your people,
and reveal the knowledge of your glory
    in the face of Jesus Christ your Son our Lord,
who is alive and reigns with you,
in the unity of the Holy Spirit,
one God, now and for ever.

 ## Talk/address/ sermon

Use the 'Faith, Hope and Love' display that was produced by the groups as a visual aid for the sermon/address (see next page). Ask the groups why they chose these particular pictures to depict the three virtues.

What do we have faith in or believe in? What do we hope for? What or whom do we love?

Discuss how Christian love, as depicted in 1 Corinthians 13, differs from the way love is viewed by the world. How does it challenge us in the way we should love each other?

Congregational/ group activities

- Produce a 'Faith, Hope and Love triptych' for use as a visual aid in the sermon. Either cut out pictures from magazines that represent one of these three virtues, or ask the groups to produce their own artwork. Fold a large board into three and label each of the sections with the name of one of the three virtues. Stick the pictures onto the appropriate part of the board. The resulting pictures could be framed like a traditional 'triptych' (a set of three painted panels usually hinged together). This is a useful art appreciation exercise if nothing else!

- Make 'Love is . . .' cards or posters, after discussing the sort of things that could be included (such as 'Love is . . . being a shoulder to cry on' or 'Love is . . . doing the washing up without being asked').

- The reading from 1 Corinthians is a challenge not only to our personal relationships, but also to how our church relates to the local community. Discuss in small groups how your church could be more effective in showing this 'agape' love in practical ways in the parish.

- Give each group several sheets of paper. Ask them to think of people in particular need of God's 'agape' love – whether these are friends, countries or groups of people – and write a prayer for them, decorating this sheet if there is time.

Prayers/ intercessions

Collect all the prayers from the groups and use these during the intercessions with the following response:

Leader　　Father of Faith, of Hope and Love:

All　　　　**in your mercy, hear us.**

Use the following thanksgiving responses:

We give thanks to God for all his gifts to us:

For birth and life and strength of body,
for safety and shelter and food,
we give you thanks, O God,
and praise your holy name.

For sight and hearing and the beauty of nature,
for words and music and the power of thought:
we give you thanks, O God,
and praise your holy name.

For work and leisure and the joy of achieving,
for conscience and will and depth of feeling:

we give you thanks, O God,
and praise your holy name.

For grace and truth in Jesus Christ,
for the gifts of the Spirit and the hope of heaven:
we give you thanks, O God,
and praise your holy name.

Holy, holy, holy Lord,
God of power and might,
heaven and earth are full of your glory,
Hosanna in the highest.

Church Family Worship (no. 478)

Stories and other resources

Patterns for Worship (pp. 100,112–13,124)

'Love', in *Pick and Mix* (p. 112)

Drama

Dave Hopwood, 'The ballad of Billy the Fool', in *A Fistful of Sketches*, NS/CHP, 1996

Music

He came down (JU p. 36)

Love one another (SHF 355)

Love beyond measure (SHF 352)

How lovely, Lord, how lovely (HON 218)

Peace is flowing like a river (HON 412, SHF 431)

The love of God (JU p. 86)

All my hope on God is founded (HAMNS 336, HON 15, HTC 451)

O Love that wilt not let me go (HON 384, HTC 486, SHF 415)

Love of the Father (HON 323)

Post communion prayer

Generous Lord,
  in word and eucharist we have proclaimed
    the mystery of your love:
  help us so to live out our days
  that we may be signs of your wonders in the
    world;
  through Jesus Christ our Saviour.

The Presentation of Christ in the Temple

Candlemas (2 February)

Candlemas is celebrated either on 2 February or on the Sunday falling between 28 January and 3 February

 ## Readings

Malachi 3.1-5

The messenger that is described in this passage is fairly clear in Christian terms as being John the Baptist. What sort of figure Malachi would have expected is another matter!

The coming of the Lord will bring a time of purification; he will be like a refiner's fire or a launderer's soap. It will result in people bringing offerings that are acceptable to God, and a time of judgement on wrongdoers.

Hebrews 2.14-18

This important reading links together the coming of Christ, his suffering and the defeat of the devil and death. His actions not only free those who were held in slavery to death, but also help him to empathize with all of us. Because he suffered when he was tempted, he can help all those who suffer temptations.

Luke 2.22-40

This reading is the same as for the Fourth Sunday of Epiphany. It describes the presentation of Jesus at the Temple and the remarkable reactions of Anna and Simeon to him.

Collect

Almighty and ever-living God,
clothed in majesty,
whose beloved Son
    was this day presented in the Temple,
in substance of our flesh:
grant that we may be presented to you
with pure and clean hearts,
by your Son Jesus Christ our Lord,
who is alive and reigns with you,
in the unity of the Holy Spirit,
one God, now and for ever.

 ## Talk/address/sermon

In advance of the service, prepare the following visual aid. Cut out a number of advertisements from magazines, e.g. adverts for cars or ice cream.

What's the message behind these adverts? What type of lifestyle are they trying to sell? What do they say you will get along with their product (more power/women/satisfaction)? How does God 'advertise' his message? What changes to lifestyle does he promise from the Malachi and Luke readings?

Congregational/ group activities

- Look at the lives of others who are sent as messengers for the faith, such as missionaries. Look at the work of one of the missionaries linked with your church, or a missionary organization. Write a message of support to them.

- Candlemas lends itself to a number of creative activities on the theme of light. Make a candle-shaped stained-glass window using black card, different coloured tissue paper and glue. Cut out the shape of a candle from the black card. Stretch and stick pieces of coloured tissue paper across the black frame. Attach the candle to a window in the church for best effect.

- This is also an opportune time to have a Christingle service. The Christingle service focuses on the image of Christ as our light. A full Christingle service is given in *The Promise of His Glory* (pp. 154–64).

 ## Prayers/ intercessions

Give each member of the congregation a candle. Ensure younger children are properly supervised and that protective candleholders are also used. Ask those sitting at the end of each pew to come forward and light their candle from the altar candle. They should then return to their pews and light the candle of the person sitting next to them. As the candles are lit, turn out the lights in the church and sing a Taizé chant such as 'Adoramus te, Domine'.

Use the following response during the intercessions:

Leader   Christ, the Light of the world:

All   **in your mercy, hear us.**

Alternatively, use the prayers for Candlemas from *The Promise of His Glory* (pp. 269–70).

 ## Stories and other resources

Candlemas ideas, in *Together with Children,* February 1996 and 1997

The Promise of His Glory (pp. 259–86)

The Candlemas sections, in *Festive Allsorts* (p. 15) and *Seasons, Saints and Sticky Tape* (p. 22)

 ## Music

Purify my heart (HON 428)

We'll sing a new song (SHF 582)

Change my heart, O God (SHF 53)

Burn, holy fire (SHF 49)

We are being built into a temple (SHF 567)

Adoramus te, Domine (HON 7, MT1 p. 42)

As pants the hart for cooling streams (HAMNS 226, HON 38)

Faithful vigil ended (HAMNS 453, HON 118, HTC 55)

Ye servants of the Lord (HAMNS 150, HON 566)

The songs used for the Fourth Sunday of Epiphany are also appropriate.

Post communion prayer

Lord, you fulfilled the hope of Simeon and Anna,
who lived to welcome the Messiah:
may we, who have received these gifts beyond words,
prepare to meet Christ Jesus when he comes
to bring us to eternal life;
for he is alive and reigns, now and for ever.

Sunday between 3 and 9 February

(if earlier than the Second Sunday before Lent)

Proper 1

Readings

Isaiah 6.1-8[9-13]

God's calling of Isaiah, the prophet. Isaiah is over-whelmed by the might and majesty in his vision of heaven. He feels doomed because he has seen God. Only those without sin may see God and live. The angel cleanses him by touching his mouth with burning coal. It is then that Isaiah answers God's call and is given his commission to warn the rebellious people of Judah.

1 Corinthians 15.1-11

Paul is writing to the people who lived in the busy port of Corinth – an important place of trade and one of the many cities of Greece. Along with Luke, Silas and Timothy, Paul spent 18 months there on his second missionary journey. There he suffered from Jewish plots against him. From the start, there were arguments amongst the believers. Paul reminds his quarrelsome readers of the truth of the gospel that he preached to them earlier. He corrects the errors they have been making in their teaching about the resurrection.

Luke 5.1-11

By the Lake of Gennesaret (called the Sea of Galilee by the other Gospel writers), Jesus teaches the crowds from Simon Peter's boat. Later they go out further into the lake and, on Jesus' instructions, they fish all night and catch such a large number of fish that their nets begin to break. What they see as Jesus' special power confirms their belief in him. The fishermen join Jesus to catch people for God.

Talk/address/ sermon

Before the service begins, cut out fish shapes from pieces of paper. Hide them around the church. Ask children to find the fish. Stick them on a board to make a fishing-net picture.

Christ wants us to 'catch people' for him. If we are to catch others, we must first act like Christ. Then we must tell others of Christ's love. How do we do this? Do we have to stand on street corners or knock on doors? In what other ways can we proclaim Christ's gospel?

Congregational/ group activities

- Cut out fish shapes from thin card or wallpaper. Decorate the fish in any way you like. Leave a space to write your name in clear, large letters. Place all the fish in a large piece of netting stretched along a wall.

- Write each statement of Paul's version of the Creed on a separate sheet of paper or card. It should be large enough to use as a visual aid.

- Jesus said, 'I will make you fishers of people.' Make a large banner or collage with this quotation. Cut out fish shapes. Place the fish on the banner or collage. Write the names of each member of the congregation on the fish, to be offered later in prayer.

Prayers/ intercessions

Use the cut-out fish shapes in the prayers today. Each person writes his or her name on a fish. Each in turn offers the fish as a sign that we offer ourselves in Christ's service. A net could be spread out over the altar to take the fish. Use the following prayer:

Heavenly Father, you know us better than we know ourselves; take these fish as a sign that we have been 'caught' for your service. Help us to give ourselves freely and completely to do your will in the world. For your sake. Amen.

Say the Nicene or baptismal creed, slowly. Pause after each statement so that it may be absorbed fully.

Stories and other resources

J. and G. Anderson, *Topsy and Tim Go Fishing*, Blackie, 1963

'Disciples', in *Pick and Mix* (p. 52)

'Jesus' friends', in *Building New Bridges* (p. 81)

Church Family Worship (no. 150)

 ## Drama

Michael Forster, 'What a catch!', in *Act One*, Kevin Mayhew, 1996

Music

An army of ordinary people (SHF 11)

God has spoken to his people (SHF 130)

Jesus called to Peter the fisherman (BBP 13)

One day when we were fishing (BBP 18)

All in an Easter Garden (CP2 130)

Bright the vision that delighted (HAMNS 96, HON 70)

Firmly I believe and truly (HAMNS 118, HON 133)

Holy, holy, holy! Lord God Almighty! (HAMNS 95, HON 212, HTC 7)

Collect and post communion prayer

Advent 2000 to Advent 2001	The Fourth Sunday before Lent on page 128
Advent 2003 to Advent 2004	The Third Sunday before Lent on page 129

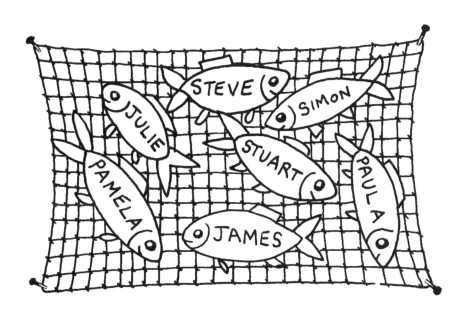

Sunday between 10 and 16 February

(if earlier than the Second Sunday before Lent)

Proper 2

 ### Readings

Jeremiah 17.5-10

In the book of Jeremiah, the young prophet attempts to warn God's people that if they continue to reject God, disaster will be inevitable. This passage is thought by some commentators to be simply a paraphrase of Psalm 1. It considers the difference between those who trust in humans and those who trust in the Lord. This is like the difference between the tree planted in the wilderness and the tree planted by the life–giving water of the river.

1 Corinthians 15.12-20

Paul sent Titus to Corinth to deal with the problems and arguments. Some of the Corinthians had been saying that there was no literal resurrection of the body. Paul states categorically that Jesus died and rose again. This is the true basis of our faith.

Luke 6.17-26

This is an echo of part of the Sermon on the Mount found in Matthew – the Beatitudes. Jesus teaches his disciples. His teaching is not exactly new to his listeners (there are similar references in the Old Testament, especially Psalms and Isaiah), but Jesus' words are contrary to those of the 'world'. Riches and popularity will not give long-lasting happiness. Those who suffer hardship in this life will have a rich reward in heaven. This is contrasted to those who would be considered well-off by the world's standards.

 ### Talk/address/ sermon

The longer version of the Beatitudes is found in Matthew Chapter 5. Matthew lists eight types of people who are blessed. Luke condenses this into four. Jesus does not promise utopia, but his words are particularly comforting to those who are rejected by society. The Dead Sea Scrolls have thrown light on the meaning of 'poor in spirit'. They are 'tender-hearted' – full of pity and mercy. There is no blessing on the hard-hearted. Jesus foretells that his followers will not be accepted by orthodox Jews.

 ### Congregational/ group activities

- Make a puppet figure of each of the apostles from a cardboard roll (covered with fabric and a piece of card for head, arms and hands). Write each of the Beatitudes on a piece of paper and stick them between the 'hands' of the apostles.

- Compare in small groups the passage from Jeremiah with Psalm 1. Do we really know what it is like to be persecuted for our faith, and to stand up for what we believe against opposition or rejection? Think of occasions in our lives or the lives of others when our faith has been tested. How did we react?

- Wrap conkers and acorns in wet cotton wool and keep them in a plastic bag. Put them in a pot to watch them grow. Alternatively, grow mustard or cress seeds.

- Look at the different Beatitude 'nouns', such as 'the meek' or 'the poor'. What does it mean to be meek?

Prayers/
intercessions

Prayers for those who try to follow Jesus' teaching:

- those who listen to the needs of others;

- those who act to help others, whatever the hardship to themselves;

- those who are persecuted for their faith.

Pray that the hearts would be turned of those who . . .

- will not listen;

- think only of themselves;

- reject or oppose those who try to follow the will of the Lord.

Use the following response:

Leader   Loving Father God

All   **help us hear your words.**

Say together this Creed from *Church Family Worship*:

Let us declare our faith in the resurrection of our Lord
   Jesus Christ:
**Christ died for our sins
in accordance with the scriptures;
he was buried;
he was raised to life on the third day
in accordance with the scriptures;
afterwards he appeared
        to his followers,
and to all the apostles:
this we have received,
        and this we believe.   Amen.**

from 1 Corinthians 15
Michael Perry, in *Church Family
Worship* (no. 256)

Stories and
other resources

Philip Welsh, 'Evil Weevil and the new school banner', in *The Reluctant Mole and Other Beastly Tales*, Scripture Union, 1979

Stories by Shirley Hughes, such as *Mr Macnally's Hat* and *Out and About*, Walker, 1983

H. J. Richards, *A Worship Anthology on the Beatitudes*, Kevin Mayhew, 1995

Church Family Worship (no. 256)

'Disciples', in *Pick and Mix* (p. 52)

The chapters on Water, in *Under Fives – Alive!* (p. 57, p. 61)

Music

I love the pit, pit, patter of the raindrops (BBP 79)

Water of life (HON 202)

Alleluia, alleluia give thanks to the risen Lord (SHF 5)

Led like a lamb to the slaughter (SHF 307)

God's not dead (JU p. 38)

This joyful Eastertide (HON 509, HTC 165)

Alleluia, alleluia, hearts to heav'n and voices raise (HAMNS 80, HON 25, HTC 151)

Blessed assurance, Jesus is mine (HON 62)

Collect and post communion prayer

Advent 2000 to Advent 2001	The Third Sunday before Lent on page 129
Advent 2003 to Advent 2004	The Proper 2 service material is not required

Sunday between 17 and 23 February

(if earlier than the Second Sunday before Lent)

Proper 3

Readings

Genesis 45.3-11,15

In Egypt Joseph is second only to Pharaoh in importance. Here he reveals his true identity to his brothers. They thought that he was long dead, or at least living as a slave for they had sold him so many years before to Egyptian merchants. Joseph appears to enjoy only a moment of revenge before he forgives his brothers. He recognizes that their actions were part of God's purpose. Through his faith, Joseph is able to save his family from starvation and destitution.

1 Corinthians 15.35-38,42-50

Paul reveals the truth of the resurrection in a comparison with plant life. The flower and the fruit have to die to allow the seed to fall into the ground and produce more flowers and fruit again next year. The new flower is different. It has its own identity. Similarly, the resurrected body is a 'spiritual' body. Adam, the first human being, represents the weak physical body. Christ, the last Adam, is a life-giving spirit. As Christians we take on the 'life-giving' mould.

Luke 6.27-38

Jesus continues to teach his disciples. He issues the great command to love – not just our friends, as anybody would, but also our enemies. In this way we must echo the love of our heavenly Father.

Talk/address/ sermon

Bring in a packet of seeds and, ideally, a full-grown plant of the same kind. Use these to illustrate the following ideas.

God's purpose is to be found in everything, even when it is hard to identify. Change and death are hard for us to cope with, but if we focus on God's everlasting love, we will find his purpose in the end. We have to change to become useful to God.

The flower is beautiful while it lasts, but this is not its only purpose. The flower dies and leaves the fruit. Inside the fruit is the seed. As the fruit rots, the seed falls to the ground. The seed grows and produces the plant which, in time, will yield yet another flower. This flower will be similar to its parent but will have an identity of its own – living in its own right.

What is love? How is it manifested? It is quite easy to love when it is reciprocated, but how do we love our enemies? Love hurts – especially when love is lost or damaged.

Congregational/ group activities

- Collect different forms of pasta and seeds to make 'pasta pictures'. Draw the shape of a flower on a piece of card and stick on different shapes of food and seeds within this flower shape.

- Cut out pictures of flowers from catalogues and stick on card (ensure there are two of each kind of flower). Play the game 'Snap' with these home-made cards.

- Make friendship bracelets (the book *All Aboard!* gives detailed instructions on how to make a variety of bracelets, such as the simple rakhi and strip Guatemalan bracelets).

- Make paper flowers, fruit and seeds to illustrate the life cycle. Stick these on a board with some of the words from the Corinthians reading such as, 'So it is with the resurrection of the dead. What is sown is perishable, what is raised is imperishable.'

- Play a game of 'If you were a flower, what kind of flower would you be?' Draw faces of the group or congregation as flowers and use these during the intercessions.

 ## Prayers/ intercessions

Use the flower drawings made during the group activities. Pray for the beautiful things in our world such as flowers, butterflies, the landscape, being able to love each other.

Leader Creator God, you made these all for us.

All **Your children give you thanks.**

Use the prayers from the sections 'Lord of Creation' in *Prayers for Children*, to focus on the beauty of God's creation. Two examples are given below:

Protection of the environment

O holy and loving Father,

you have created for us a wonderful world:
please forgive us when we cause harm
to your creation
and teach us how to love and cherish
everything that has life,
that our world may remain
a place of beauty and boundless glory,
now and for ever.

Plant life

For the softness of moss,
we thank you, O Lord.
For the strength of the oak tree,
we thank you, O Lord.
For the fragrance of roses,
we thank you, O Lord.
For all the plants in all of the world,
we thank you, O Lord.

*Prayers for Children
(nos. 79, p. 56 and 76, p. 55)*

 ## Stories and other resources

Anita Haigh, 'Bully for you!', in *Rap, Rhyme and Reason*, Scripture Union, 1996

Christopher Herbert, *Prayers for Children*, NS/CHP, 1993

Patterns for Worship (p. 111)

'The garden centre', in *Under Fives – Alive!* (p. 49)

'Love', in *Pick and Mix* (p. 112)

The material on friendship bracelets, in *All Aboard!* (Section 2:03)

 ## Music

To ev'rything, turn, turn, turn (CP2 113)

Now the green blade rises (CP2 131)

Love will never come to an end (CP2 99)

Give us hope, Lord (CP2 87)

A new commandment (SHF 14)

Love one another (SHF 355)

Praise to the holiest in the height (HAMNS 117, HON 426, HTC 140, SHF 450)

Love to the Father (HON 323)

My Lord, you wore no royal crown (HTC 118)

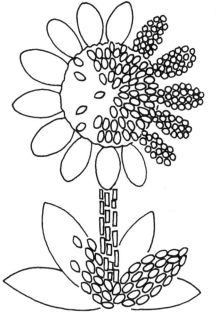

Collect and Post communion prayer

Advent 2000 to Advent 2001	The Proper 3 service material is not required for these years
Advent 2003 to Advent 2004	

The Second Sunday Before Lent

Readings

Genesis 2.4b-9,15-25

This is the second creation story in Genesis. Adam is made from the 'dust of the ground' and placed in the perfect garden of Eden. Here he has charge over the animals and has everything he needs. The only thing that he must not touch is the 'tree of the knowledge of good and evil'. In his great love for his creation, God provides everything that the man needs, including a companion of his own kind – a woman.

Revelation 4

The traditional view is that John, one of the sons of Zebedee, is the writer of the book of Revelation. At this time in the history of the early Church, Christ's followers are beginning to suffer persecution as they refuse to obey the law to worship the Roman emperor. John writes to encourage those early Christians to stand firm. His vision of heaven reflects that of Isaiah: it reveals the glory of God. The scene is set for the final conflict with the forces of evil. Those who love God need have no fear.

Luke 8.22-25

Jesus tries to snatch a few minutes' peace as his fishermen friends take him across the lake. Lake Gennesaret (the Sea of Galilee) is prone to sudden, violent storms. This appears to be a particularly violent squall as the disciples, despite being experienced fishermen, fail to manage by themselves. In their panic they wake Jesus. Jesus reveals that by faith he is able to calm the storm. If they had not been certain before, they now recognize that Jesus is no ordinary man.

Collect

Almighty God,
you have created the heavens and the earth
and made us in your own image:
teach us to discern your hand in all your works
and your likeness in all your children;
through Jesus Christ your Son our Lord,
who with you and the Holy Spirit
 reigns supreme over all things,
now and for ever.

Talk/address/ sermon

In our difficult times we may shout at God: 'What are you doing to help me? Why have you left me alone when I needed you most?' Use Psalm 22 and Jesus' cry from the cross here. It is at such times as these that many people have felt most comforted by God. Even though we might feel God is distant from us, he remains constantly with us – his protective arm surrounding us even when we are unaware of his presence. Use the Footprints poem or stories of coping with suffering, such as Margaret Spufford's *Celebration* (Fount, 1989).

Congregational/ group activities

*   The Footprints poem reminds us that God is always with us and particularly when we are most vulnerable. Read the poem. Cut out shapes of footprints. Draw pictures or write words on the footprints to show when God has carried us through bad times. Place them on the ground to make a path.

*   Discuss in groups: how do we cope with difficult times? What can help us when we struggle? What have other people done that has helped us, and how can we help others?

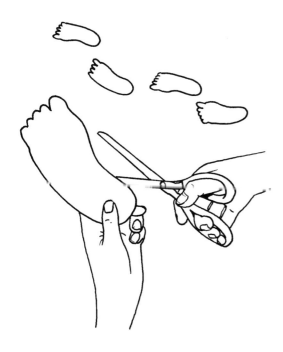

Stories and other resources

Patterns for Worship (p. 188)

Christopher Herbert, 'Lord of Creation', in *Prayers for Children*, NS/CHP, 1993

'The storm at sea', in *Praise, Play and Paint* (p. 38)

'Journeys', in *Pick and Mix* (p. 96)

Drama

Dave Hopwood, 'In the beginning', in *Acting Up*, NS/CHP, 1995

Music

One day when we were fishing (BBP 18)

Worthy, O worthy are you Lord (SHF 624)

Jesus is Lord! (SHF 278)

You are worthy (SHF 634)

O Lord, my God (HON 380, SHF 407)

All people that on earth do dwell (HAMNS 100, HTC 14, SHF 8)

Eternal Father, strong to save (HAMNS 292, HON 114, HTC 285)

- Read together the legend of St Christopher (this is retold in the chapter on Journeys in *Pick and Mix*). Make a St Christopher badge from play-dough or clay.

- Give people a sheet of paper. Ask them to write down the name of someone to pray for, or something to pray for themselves. Collect the pieces of paper into a large box.

Prayers/ intercessions

Use the prayers written during the activity time as the prayers of intercession. Finish the time of prayer with the following responses:

Leader	The Lord God almighty is our Father:
All	**he loves us and tenderly cares for us.**
Leader	The Lord Jesus Christ is our Saviour:
All	**he has redeemed us and will defend us to the end.**
Leader	The Lord, the Holy Spirit, is among us:
All	**he will lead us in God's holy way. To God almighty, Father, Son and Holy Spirit, be praise and glory today and for ever. Amen.**

Trevor Lloyd, in *Patterns for Worship* (p. 188)

Post communion prayer

God our creator,
by your gift
the tree of life was set at the heart of the earthly paradise,
and the bread of life at the heart of your Church:
may we who have been nourished at your table on earth
be transformed by the glory of the Saviour's cross
and enjoy the delights of eternity;
through Jesus Christ our Lord.

The Sunday Next Before Lent

 ## Readings

Exodus 34.29-35

Moses returns from his encounter with God on Mount Sinai and reveals God's commands. He is profoundly affected by this meeting, reflecting the glory he has witnessed. His face becomes radiant every time he enters the Lord's presence but he covers his face with a veil when in the presence of the Israelites.

2 Corinthians 3.12 – 4.2

The Corinthians are suffering from impostors who preach a false gospel. Paul reveals the effect of the gospel truth. When Moses encountered God, he had to veil his face because the effect of the glory faded. The new covenant, however, as revealed by Jesus and reflected by his followers, is so glorious that it increases as we become more like Christ.

Luke 9.28-36[37-43]

Jesus takes Peter, James and John up the mountain to pray (traditionally this is on Mount Tabor, but could be Mount Hermon). The three disciples here witness the appearance of Moses and Elijah who speak with Jesus. Jesus' face changes. In his usual impulsive manner, Peter wants to build three shelters for Moses, Elijah and Jesus. God speaks and confirms that Jesus is his chosen Son. After the voice has spoken, the disciples find Jesus alone.

Collect

Almighty Father,
whose Son was revealed in majesty
before he suffered death upon the cross:
give us grace to perceive his glory,
that we may be strengthened to suffer with him
and be changed into his likeness, from glory to
   glory;
who is alive and reigns with you,
in the unity of the Holy Spirit,
one God, now and for ever.

 ## Talk/address/ sermon

Use the pictures that the groups produced earlier in the service (see first activity below).

As these pictures show, there are a variety of occasions and ways that people have felt God's presence. In today's readings, the remarkable presence of God was felt by both Moses and the disciples. Why was it important in the Gospel reading for Jesus to be singled out in such a manner? How would his disciples have felt when witnessing Jesus' transfiguration?

 ## Congregational/ group activities

- Discuss the times when the group have most felt God's presence. Was this while viewing an awe-inspiring part of his creation, during a crowded and lively service, or during a quiet time of prayer? Draw or paint a picture of a time when people have been aware of God's presence and use this at the beginning of the talk.

- Produce a banner with the words from the Gospel reading: 'This is my Son, my Chosen; listen to him.'

- Prepare for the beginning of Lent this week. Discuss the reasons why we observe Lent. Think of positive things that could be taken up for Lent, including giving more time to prayer. Give each person in the group two pieces of paper. Ask them to fold these together, to make an eight-sided booklet. Put the title of Lent on the cover page. Write in the names, or draw pictures, of seven topics or people to pray for during Lent – one for each day of the week.

 Prayers/ intercessions

Use some slides of beautiful landscapes, babies, animals, and anything else that can remind us of God's wonderful creation. Use the following responses:

We thank God for the wonderful world he has given to us, and for all his love and care:

For the warmth of the sun: O loving Father,
we give you thanks and praise.

For the rain which makes things grow: O loving Father,
we give you thanks and praise.

For the woods and the fields: O loving Father,
we give you thanks and praise.

For the sea and the sky: O loving Father,
we give you thanks and praise.

For the flowers and the animals: O loving Father,
we give you thanks and praise.

For families and holidays: O loving Father,
we give you thanks and praise.

For all your gifts: O loving Father,
we give you thanks and praise. Amen.

Michael Perry, in *Church Family Worship,* no. 364

Stories and other resources

Christopher Herbert, 'The Seasons' section, in *Prayers for Children*, NS/CHP, 1993

Transfiguration section, in *Festive Allsorts* (p. 46)

Patterns for Worship (p. 124)

Music

Jesus shall take the highest honour (HON 278)

Majesty, worship his majesty (SHF 358)

Look and see the glory of the King (SHF 333)

Lord, the light of your love is shining (HON 317)

The King is among us (HON 483, SHF 511)

At the name of Jesus (HAMNS 148, HON 46, HTC 172, SHF 26)

Christ, whose glory fills the skies (HAMNS 4, HON 82, HTC 266)

Hail, thou once despisèd Jesus (HON 192, HTC 175, SHF 145)

Post communion prayer

Holy God,
we see your glory in the face of Jesus Christ:
may we who are partakers at his table
reflect his life in word and deed,
that all the world may know
  his power to change and save.
This we ask through Jesus Christ our Lord.

The First Sunday of Lent

Readings

Deuteronomy 26.1-11

Here is part of the Law given by Moses to the Israelites as they approached the Promised Land concerning the harvest offerings. The offering was to be a basket of the choicest first fruits given to God, an acknowledgement that God is the giver of all good gifts. The ceremony was to continue with a prayer of remembrance of how God had delivered and protected the Israelites and brought them into a new land. The harvest offering was to be made in return for God's goodness.

Romans 10.8b-13

Paul reminds us that if we confess with our lips that Jesus is Lord and believe that God raised him from the dead we shall be saved. Paul encourages the Philippians that it is by faith that we are put right with God. We are called to confess to one another the ways of God and the truth about his Son Jesus Christ. God is the same Lord who richly blesses all; he holds no distinction between class and colour.

Luke 4.1-13

Here is the story of the temptations of Jesus in the wilderness at the start of his earthly ministry. Jesus responds to Satan's taunts by using the words from Deuteronomy (8.3; 6.16; 6.13). These key passages of Scripture reflect the 40-year history of the Israelites' disobedience to God in the wilderness. Jesus remains faithful to his calling and his heavenly Father. When Satan realizes this he leaves Jesus alone.

Collect

Almighty God,
whose Son Jesus Christ fasted forty days in the wilderness,
and was tempted as we are, yet without sin:
give us grace to discipline ourselves
    in obedience to your Spirit;
and, as you know our weakness,
so may we know your power to save;
through Jesus Christ your Son our Lord,
who is alive and reigns with you,
in the unity of the Holy Spirit,
one God, now and for ever.

Talk/address/ sermon

On a flipchart or large sheet of paper write a scenario which requires a choice to be made e.g. 'You are late for an appointment and the only parking space is marked 'disabled'. Do you . . . ?' On three pieces of card write three possible solutions and invite three people to read out the choices. Repeat with a second scenario. Talk about the temptations of Jesus and how they were particular to him. We need to recognize the subtlety of temptation in making choices between what is good or bad, right or wrong. Talk about the images of Satan – person dressed in red with horns (using various cartoon pictures if you have them). Such images may cause us to dismiss Satan and his power. The Bible talks about Satan being like a prowling lion, an angel of light, a serpent. Jesus knows what it is to be tempted. He understands and still loves us even when we get it wrong.

Congregational/ group activities

- Hold a pancake party and explore what the 40 days of Lent are about.

- Think about spring cleaning. Lent is like a spiritual spring clean. Draw a collection of cleaning utensils: mop, duster, vacuum cleaner, brush, etc. On each one think of something we might want to look at in our lives, e.g. prayer, spending time with God, being kind, being helpful . . .

- Suggest that rather than give something up for Lent we might think of something extra to do to help us think about God.

- In groups make a list of the top ten temptations that we all face today. Talk about what helps you to make right choices. When might it be difficult to make the 'right' choice for yourself, or for others?

- Using newspapers and magazines make a montage of pictures that reflect the sins of the world – greed, hatred, war, anger, jealousy. Use these as a focus for the intercessions. Give each person a small piece of paper and invite everyone to write something they would like God to help them change in their life. What would they change in the world, if they could choose?

- Make a Lenten tree. Cut out the shape of a large tree from brown paper or card. Stick this onto backing paper, on a display board. Ask children to draw pictures based on the Gospel readings for each week and stick these to the branches of the tree.

 ## Prayers/ intercessions

(*The responses are based on Psalm 91.14-16. Read these verses at the beginning of the intercessions.*)

Pray for all going through a time of temptation.
Pray for a growing trust in God.
Pray for a Church that stands for what is true.
Pray for those in leadership, that they may not abuse their position of power.
Pray for all who are sick or in any kind of need.

After each prayer use the response:

Leader   God says:
All   **When you call to me, I will answer you.**
   When you are in trouble, I will be with you.

or

Use a Taizé sung response:

O Lord hear my prayer
O Lord hear my prayer
When I call answer me.

O Lord hear my prayer
O Lord hear my prayer
Come and listen to me.

(Psalm 101)

 ## Stories and other resources

Music from Taizé (Vol. 2), HarperCollins, 1985

'Choices', in *Pick and Mix* (p. 31)

'Lent' (p. 22) and 'St Martin' (p. 57) in *Festive Allsorts*

Christopher Herbert, Lent prayers, in *Prayers for Children*, NS/CHP, 1993

Drama

Dave Hopwood, 'Don't touch', in *A Fistful of Sketches*, NS/CHP, 1996

 ## Music

Within our darkest night (Taizé song – HON 562)

Hallelujah my Father (SHF 149)

Rejoice! Rejoice! (SHF 461)

O Lord, hear my prayer (HON 379, MT2 p. 46)

Forty days and forty nights in Judah's desert (HON 144)

God of grace and God of glory (HAMNS 367, HON 174, HTC 324)

Lead us, heav'nly Father, lead us (HAMNS 224, HON 293, HTC 525)

Forty days and forty nights (HAMNS 56, HON 145, HTC 103)

Post communion prayer

Lord God,
you have renewed us with the living bread from heaven;
by it you nourish our faith,
increase our hope,
and strengthen our love:
teach us always to hunger for him
who is the true and living bread,
and enable us to live by every word
that proceeds from out of your mouth;
through Jesus Christ our Lord.

The Second Sunday of Lent

 ## Readings

Genesis 15.1-12,17,18

God promises Abram that he will have a son to be his heir, and that, as many as the stars are in the heavens, so will be Abram's descendants. Abram trusts God to fulfil his promise.

Philippians 3.17 – 4.1

Paul writes to the Philippians urging them to imitate his own style of Christian living and to stand firm in the faith. He warns them against giving in to self-indulgence and earthly things. He reminds them that when Christ comes again, he will transform our earthly bodies, with all their weaknesses, into his own glorious body.

Luke 13.31-35

Jesus is threatened by Herod, but Jesus pays little attention. He knows what lies ahead of him and grieves only for the city and its people who will destroy him. He reflects his love for Jerusalem in the picture of the mother hen who gathers her chicks under her wing. *'How many times have I wanted to put my arms around all your people, but you would not let me.'*

Collect

Almighty God,
you show to those who are in error the light of
    your truth,
that they may return to the way of righteousness:
grant to all those who are admitted
    into the fellowship of Christ's religion,
that they may reject those things
    that are contrary to their profession,
and follow all such things as are agreeable to the
    same;
through our Lord Jesus Christ,
who is alive and reigns with you,
in the unity of the Holy Spirit,
one God, now and for ever.

 ## Talk/address/ sermon

Think about people who protect us and care for us. Use pictures or OHPs, or members of the congregation dressed up, e.g. doctors, nurses, firemen, parents, friends.

Who looks after us at home, in school, at work, in the local community? How can we show care and protection to one another? How does it feel when that love is rejected? Discuss the Gospel reading and how Jesus wept over Jerusalem.

Play a game of 'Simon Said' to think about how we imitate or copy one another. Some things are good to imitate, others are not so good.

What does Paul urge the Philippians to imitate?

Prepare two OHP transparencies, one with a paper gingerbread person shape in the centre, and the other the same outline coloured in with OHP pens so that the light shines through the shape. Talk about our weaknesses that often influence us to make wrong choices (place paper shape on OHP). Replace with coloured acetate to illustrate how Jesus will change our mortal bodies to reflect his glorious body.

 ## Congregational/ group activities

- Play the 'Protection game'. Collect or draw a number of pictures showing people caring and protecting. Cut the pictures in half and mix them with other pictures of people being hurt or uncared for. Ask the groups to match the caring pictures and stick them onto a large sheet of paper entitled 'People who Care'. Talk about the people who protect and care for us.

- Have an outline of a large mother hen. Using fabrics, feathers and wool, let the children make a collage of the hen. Talk about protection – what does it mean? Discuss in the groups how Jesus used the picture of the mother hen and her chicks to show how he wants to love and protect us. Give each person a small cut-out shape of a chick and invite them to colour it in and write their name on it. Stick the chicks with the mother hen onto some card as a visual for the service.

Stories and other resources

Leslie Francis and Nicola Slee, *The Walk: Out and About with Teddy Horsley*, NCEC, 1990

Philip Welsh, 'Herbert the Hedgehog's new sister', in *The Reluctant Mole and Other Beastly Tales*, Scripture Union, 1979

'New babies', in *Under Fives – Alive!* (p. 17)

Drama

Michael Forster, 'Whatever you've done, I love you', *Act One*, Kevin Mayhew, 1996

 **Music**

Father, I place into your hands (SHF 94)

Nada te turbe (Taizé song – HON 347)

Have you seen the pussycat? (JU p. 64)

He made the stars to shine (JU p. 70)

You laid aside your majesty (SHF 638)

Take up thy cross (HAMNS 237, HTC 114)

The Lord's my shepherd (HAMNS 426, HON 490, HTC 591, SHF 526)

The King of love my shepherd is (HAMNS 126, HON 484, HTC 44, SHF 513)

- In groups, list the ways Jesus shows his love and protection for us. Alongside that list make another one describing the kind of ways we can respond to that love.

- Give everyone two circles of paper or two people-shaped pieces of paper. (Use gingerbread biscuit cutters for the outline.) Invite them to write the name of or draw someone they would like to place in Jesus' protective arms. Ask them to write their name (or draw themselves) on the second piece of paper. This activity will then be used during a time of prayer.

- Add more pictures to the Lenten tree.

Prayers/ intercessions

During some quiet music or singing the children could collect up the shapes that were made during the all-age activity and Blu-Tack them onto a large sheet of paper with a simple outline of hands or arms.

Thank God for his protective love.
Pray for those who reject God's love.
Pray for Jerusalem, a city still besieged by conflict.

Post communion prayer

Almighty God,
you see that we have no power of ourselves to
    help ourselves:
keep us both outwardly in our bodies,
and inwardly in our souls;
that we may be defended from all adversities
    which may happen to the body,
and from all evil thoughts
    which may assault and hurt the soul;
through Jesus Christ our Lord.

The Third Sunday of Lent

 ## Readings

Isaiah 55.1-9

This call to those in need is warm and personal, reaching to the basics of human need. It is echoed again by Jesus in John 6.35 ('I am the bread of life . . .'). In the same way that God promises to satisfy all our needs, so he calls for repentance, to leave behind the old ways of life and to turn to God for his forgiveness and mercy.

1 Corinthians 10.1-13

Paul speaks to the Corinthian church reminding them of how the Israelites tested God in the desert and turned from his ways. Paul exhorts the Corinthian church to be careful in case they too fall into sinful ways. We can be confident that no temptation is too great to overcome. God promises to be with us when we trust him.

Luke 13.1-9

Roman troops had slaughtered some Galilean pilgrims in the Temple at Passover. The people assumed that the victims must have been especially wicked. Jesus tells the people that these Galileans were not worse sinners because of what happened to them. He warns the people against such thinking and suggests that unless they turn from their sins they too will die in the same way. Jesus goes on to tell them the parable of the unfruitful fig tree.

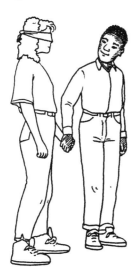

Collect

Almighty God,
whose most dear Son went not up to joy
   but first he suffered pain,
and entered not into glory before he was crucified:
mercifully grant that we, walking in the way of the
   cross,
may find it none other than the way of life and
   peace;
through Jesus Christ your Son our Lord,
who is alive and reigns with you,
in the unity of the Holy Spirit,
one God, now and for ever.

 ## Talk/address/ sermon

Use a pair of walking boots, drinks bottle, walking stick, guide book or map and a compass as visual aids.

How can we decide which is the right way to go? We can follow a map, or read the signposts. Even if we have a map we may still need a compass to know which direction to go in.

Jesus is like our compass pointing the way to follow. The Bible is like a map giving directions and signs on the way. The Bible can help us to know what to do when we go the wrong way.

Have several pieces of paper ready shaded in different ways – light grey, dark grey and black. The gospel is not about grades of awfulness but about God's mercy, forgiveness and provision. There will always be conflict between what is good and what is evil. God can give us hope in the struggle. Just as these pieces of paper are shaded in different ways, do we try to grade sins?

Set out an obstacle course in church. Blindfold an older child or adult and carefully direct them around this course. Life can be like this obstacle course, as we struggle to choose between what is right and wrong. Yet we don't have to remain blindfolded. God has given us different guides to help us through life (discuss the role of the Holy Spirit, prayer, the Bible and other Christians in helping us through life).

Congregational/ group activities

- Ask the groups to take off their shoes and put them back on the wrong feet. Tell them to walk around the room and to say how it feels. When we put our shoes on the wrong feet it feels uncomfortable – when we do something wrong it can make us feel uncomfortable inside. We can put our shoes on the right feet to feel more comfortable – we can ask God to forgive us so that we can feel right again on the inside.

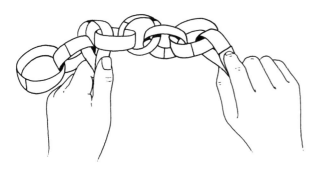

- Give everybody a coloured strip of paper which can be joined together to make a chain. Invite everybody to write something on the strip of paper which they want to ask God's forgiveness for. Join all the pieces of paper together and ask everyone to stand inside the chain. Explain that when we do wrong we can often become trapped. God wants to free us as we turn to him. Invite everyone to burst out of the chain. Link into the prayers.

- Add more pictures to the Lenten tree.

 # Prayers/ intercessions

This is an action prayer to help the congregation to use their whole bodies in prayer. This could lead into saying the Peace.

When we do wrong we hurt ourselves
point to self
When we do wrong we hurt others
look around congregation
When we do wrong we hurt God
point upwards
We need to say, 'Sorry'
head bowed, silence, then quietly say sorry in own time.

God in his love forgives us
lift heads
He washes us clean
raise hands
He sets us free to love one another
shake hands with those around
Together we say, 'Thank you God'

 # Stories and other resources

Leslie Francis and Nicola Slee, *The Grumpy Day*, NCEC, 1994

'Forgiveness', in *Pick and Mix* (p. 64)

 # Drama

Dave Hopwood, 'The bagman', in *A Fistful of Sketches*, NS/CHP, 1996

 # Music

God forgave my sin in Jesus' name (SHF 126)

I'm sorry, I'm sorry (FG p. 23)

O Lord, all the world belongs to you (HON 378)

Senhor, tem piedade de nós (WP 66)

I get so excited, Lord (SHF 189)

Amazing grace! (HON 27, HTC 28, SHF 10)

Jesu, grant me this, I pray (HON 260)

Put thou thy trust in God (HAMNS 223, HON 429)

Post communion prayer

Merciful Lord,
grant your people grace to withstand the temptations of the world, the flesh and the devil,
and with pure hearts and minds to follow you, the only God;
through Jesus Christ our Lord.

The Third Sunday of Lent

Mothering Sunday

The Fourth Sunday of Lent

 ## Readings

Exodus 2.1-10

Moses is hidden for three months from the Egyptian soldiers. Finally, his mother places him in a papyrus basket and puts him in the reeds along the bank of the Nile. He is found by Pharaoh's daughter.

or

1 Samuel 1.20-28

Hannah gives birth to a son and names him Samuel. He is taken to Eli and offered to the Lord's service.

2 Corinthians 1.3-7

Paul writes of how God is a comfort to us in all our troubles. However, we are helped in order that we can help others.

or

Colossians 3.12-17

As God's chosen people we are exhorted to clothe ourselves with compassion, tenderness, humility, gentleness and patience. We are also commanded to forgive as the Lord forgave us.

Luke 2.33-35

Simeon prophesies about the coming life of Jesus and foretells that Mary's own soul will be pierced with a sword.

or

John 19.25-27

Jesus' mother stands at the foot of the cross. Even in his great pain Jesus shows concern for his mother and entrusts her into the care of his beloved disciple, John.

Collect

God of compassion,
    whose Son Jesus Christ, the child of Mary,
    shared the life of a home in Nazareth,
    and on the cross drew the whole human family to
        himself:
    strengthen us in our daily living
    that in joy and in sorrow
    we may know the power of your presence
        to bind together and to heal;
    through Jesus Christ your Son our Lord,
    who is alive and reigns with you,
    in the unity of the Holy Spirit,
    one God, now and for ever.

Talk/address/ sermon

Invite two or three mothers to the front with one of their children. Blindfold the mothers and ask them questions about their child, e.g. the length of hair, colour of eyes, favourite food. Now ask them by touch alone to distinguish their child from the others. Talk about how God knows and loves each one of us with all our differences, referring to Isaiah 49.15.

Look at the role Mary played as the mother of Jesus. Use silhouette pictures of a baby, a young boy, a man, and Jesus on the cross. Refer to Simeon's prophecy (Luke 2.34-35), Jesus lost at the Temple in Jerusalem (Luke 2.49), the wedding at Cana (John 2.5), Mary at the cross (John 19.25-27).

Julian of Norwich said: *'As truly as God is Father, so just as truly is he our mother.'*

Focus on the fact that everyone has, or has had a mother. Acknowledge that everyone will have had a different experience, some might be painful. God is the perfect parent.

Congregational/ group activities

- As the people arrive, help them to make masks out of paper plates of the characters in the story of the prodigal son (including some pigs). The people can act out the story as it is read, using the masks they have made. This could be shown during the service, maybe as the Gospel reading.

- The prodigal son's father threw a party to celebrate and welcome his son home. Talk about other times that we celebrate with a party. Discuss the importance of Mothering Sunday as a celebration. Let the children ice biscuits to share with the rest of the congregation.

- Talk about how we are all different and yet how God knows and loves each one of us. Let each child make a flower out of tissue paper and a pipe cleaner. Try and use as many different colours as possible. Explain to the children that they are going to use their flowers to make a flower arrangement in church to show how God loves and knows each one of us. After the service the children can be encouraged to give their flowers to their mothers. If there is enough time, extra flowers could be made to give to other people in the congregation.

- Using a long narrow roll of paper put a time line around the church divided up into decades. Invite people to go and stand within the decade in which they were born. Talk in these groups about the things they remember about that time. Invite one person from each decade to share with everyone something about that period. One thing we all have in common is that God knows us and has known us from the womb (refer to Psalm 139.15,16).

- Divide the congregation into five groups and give each group one of the Mary readings used in the address/sermon. Invite them to talk about how it would have felt for Mary and then create a 'still frame' pose of the passage. Each group could take up their still frame to show the other groups, giving a feeling of Mary's place as mother in Jesus' life.

Prayers/ intercessions

Use the thoughts around Mary the mother of Jesus as a framework for the prayers. Read out these Bible verses and pray for the themes mentioned below.

Luke 1.38	Mary's obedience to God
	Pray that we too might be obedient
Luke 2.33	Mary's treasuring of Simeon's words
	Pray for the nations of the world

Luke 2.48	Mary's anxiety and anger
	Pray for those who are anxious
John 2.5	Mary's trust in her son
	Pray that we may learn to trust
John 19.25	Mary's pain at the cross
	Pray for those in pain

Invite a range of people of different ages to lead the intercessions, using prayers from *Patterns for Worship* (such as Prayers for the Family on p. 83).

Stories and other resources

'The lost son', *Palm Tree Bible*, Palm Tree Press, 1992

Julian of Norwich, *Enfolded in Love,* Darton, Longman and Todd, 1980

The chapter on Mothering Sunday, in *Praise, Play and Paint* (p. 60)

Drama

Derek Haylock, 'As a mother', in *Plays for all Seasons*, NS/CHP, 1997

Ruth Tiller, 'Consider the birds of the air', and 'Thank you, Mum!', in *Keeping the Feast*, Kevin Mayhew, 1995

Music

I am a new creation (SHF 179)

O Lord, all the world belongs to you (HON 378)

There are hundreds of sparrows (JP 246)

The steadfast love of the Lord (SHF 541)

Living under the shadow of his wing (SHF 331)

At the cross her station keeping (HAMNS 69, HON 44)

O worship the King, all glorious above (HAMNS 101, HON 393, SHF 428)

Praise, my soul, the King of heaven (HAMNS 192, HON 422, SHF 441)

Post communion prayer

Loving God,
as a mother feeds her children at the breast
you feed us in this sacrament
    with the food and drink of eternal life:
help us who have tasted your goodness
to grow in grace within the household of faith;
through Jesus Christ our Lord.

The Fifth Sunday of Lent

 ## Readings

Isaiah 43.16-21

The Lord tells the Israelites to cling no longer to the past, but to watch for a new thing that he will bring about. The Lord will make a way in the desert, a new path on which they will be led.

Philippians 3.4b-14

In his letter to the Philippians Paul urges them to set their faith in the Lord Jesus Christ. He reflects on how he obeyed the commands of the Law to gain a righteousness of his own, one based on his actions. Paul reflects how he has thrown all that away to receive the righteousness that comes from God, one that is based on faith alone. All he wants is 'to know Christ and the power of his resurrection'. His goal now is to look forward and strive towards the hope of being raised himself from death to life.

John 12.1-8

Jesus is anointed at Bethany by Mary. She anoints his feet with very expensive perfume and wipes them with her hair. Judas Iscariot is angry that the perfume had not been sold and the money given to the poor. Jesus defends Mary's actions and praises her for her love. He links her action to the anointing of his body, for what is his impending death.

Collect

> Most merciful God,
> who by the death and resurrection of your Son
>   Jesus Christ
> delivered and saved the world:
> grant that by faith in him who suffered on the
>   cross
> we may triumph in the power of his victory;
> through Jesus Christ your Son our Lord,
> who is alive and reigns with you,
> in the unity of the Holy Spirit,
> one God, now and for ever.

 ## Talk/address/ sermon

Prepare the following visual aids (which could be pictures or the genuine article): a bottle of expensive perfume, a cross, a large footprint or running baton.

How do you show someone that you love and care for them? Usually this is through kindness, gifts, or expressions of love.

Bottle of perfume (from the Gospel reading). Mary showed her love by anointing Jesus with an expensive gift of perfume.

Cross. Jesus showed his love by dying for us on the cross.

Large footprint or running baton (from the Epistle). Paul showed his love by living his life getting to know Jesus better and telling others about him.

How can we show our love to Jesus?

 ## Congregational/ group activities

- On a large outline of a hand, write all the ways that people can show us they love and care for us. Draw round your own hand and think of five ways you could help others. Write or draw one idea in each finger.

- Make a list, or draw all the people who care for us (parents, friends, relatives and members of the

caring professions such as teachers, doctors, etc.). Mount these pictures on card, to be displayed in church. What do they do to show their love?

- Tell the story (or act it out) of Mary anointing Jesus' feet. Discuss why it was a strange way to show love. How might you show your love to Jesus?

- Divide the congregation into small groups and ask them to stand in small circles. (Quiet music could be played.) Give one person in each circle a small pot of perfumed oil. Each member of the group marks a cross on the palm of the hand of the person next to them, with the words, 'Christ's love is for you.' The oil is then passed on to the next person. End the time with the words altogether 'We are the body of Christ. By one Spirit we were all baptized into one body. Keep the unity of the Spirit in the bond of peace.' Share the Peace with other groups.

- Complete the Lenten tree pictures.

Prayers/ intercessions

Use the symbols of the perfume, cross and footstep as a focus for the prayers.

Perfume: Pray for ways we can show other people Christ's love.

Pray for Christ's anointing and healing of the sick.

Cross: Thank God for Christ's love which took him to the cross.

Bring to the cross the sins of the world.

Footstep: Pray that as a church we may follow Christ.

Pray that we may be witnesses for Christ wherever we are.

Alternatively, use these responses to focus on our need for renewal and for God's forgiveness:

O God, we come to you in repentance,
conscious of our sins;

When we are self-satisfied, you expose our failure.
Lord, forgive us:
save us and help us.

When we are self-assertive, you challenge our pride.
Lord, forgive us:
save us and help us.

When we are self-opinionated, you show us we do not know everything.
Lord, forgive us:
save us and help us.

When we are self-indulgent, you condemn our greed.
Lord, forgive us:
save us and help us.

When we are self-centred, you take our peace away.
Lord, forgive us:
save us and help us.

Give us a new vision of your holiness,
make us worthy to be your people,
and help us to live up to our calling
in Jesus Christ our Lord. Amen.

Church Family Worship (no. 465)

Stories and other resources

Susan Varley, *Badger's Parting Gift*, Collins, 1984

Doris Stickney, *Water Bugs and Dragonflies*, Mowbray, 1997

Jim Dainty, *Mudge, Gill and Steve*, NS/CHP, 1997

Church Family Worship (no. 465)

'Forgiveness', in *Pick and Mix* (p. 64)

 ## Music

I want to walk with Jesus Christ (JP 124)

O Lord, all the world belongs to you (HON 378)

I want to worship the Lord (SHF 247)

Your love for me is a mystery (SHF 639)

We sing the praise of him who died (HAMNS 138, HON 536, HTC 146)

Glory be to Jesus (HON 159, HTC 126)

It is a thing most wonderful (HAMNS 70, HON 255, HTC 131)

Post communion prayer

Lord Jesus Christ,
you have taught us
that what we do for the least of our brothers and sisters
we do also for you:
give us the will to be the servant of others
as you were the servant of all,
and gave up your life and died for us,
but are alive and reign, now and for ever.

Palm Sunday

Readings

Liturgy of the Palms

Luke 19.28-40

Jesus knew that as he rode into Jerusalem he was taking a double risk. He chose to ride on a donkey, thus announcing his intention of coming in peace rather than as a warrior to make war. Symbolically Jesus was saying, 'I come as your King in love and peace – will you take me as your King?' In choosing to do this he was risking rejection and death. The cheering crowds were soon to change their cry of 'Hosanna' to one of 'Crucify'.

Liturgy of the Passion

Isaiah 50.4-9a

The passage tells of the unnamed servant's great obedience to the Lord, faithfully serving him through times of great persecution. The servant is clearly linked with Jesus, in the descriptions of the mocking, spitting and beating that Jesus also faced before his crucifixion.

Philippians 2.5-11

Paul encourages the Philippians to continue in the faith. He urges them to take on the attitude and ways of Christ, who bore the very nature of God, yet gave up all that he had and became man. He took on himself the form of a servant and throughout his life he was obedient to his Father, even to death on a cross. Through his obedience, God raised him up and gave him the name above all names, that all may worship him.

or

Luke 22.14 – 23.56

This extended Gospel reading includes the events of the Last Supper, Jesus' prayer on the Mount of Olives, his arrest and Peter's denial. It concludes with Jesus' crucifixion and burial. (*Provision is also made for a shorter Gospel reading of Luke 23.1-49.*)

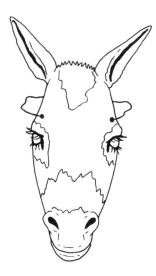

Collect

Almighty and everlasting God,
who in your tender love towards the human race
    sent your Son our Saviour Jesus Christ
to take upon him our flesh
and to suffer death upon the cross:
grant that we may follow the example
    of his patience and humility,
and also be made partakers of his resurrection;
through Jesus Christ your Son our Lord,
who is alive and reigns with you,
in the unity of the Holy Spirit,
one God, now and for ever.

Talk/address/ sermon

Explore the changing emotions of the journey into Jerusalem, from the cheering crowd, to Jesus weeping over the city, to the anger at the money changers in the Temple courtyard. Play extracts from different pieces of music which reflect different moods. *How does the music make you feel? What other things affect how we feel?* Go on to explore the changing emotions of the crowd towards Jesus.

Congregational/ group activities

- Send the children on a donkey hunt (a real donkey, cardboard cut-out, toy donkey or donkey mask could be hidden). Give the children a series of clues to follow, like Jesus gave to the disciples. The found donkey could then form part of the procession to church.

- Make donkey masks from card or paper plates. The children could wear these in a Palm Sunday procession.

- Make brightly coloured streamers from ribbons or crêpe paper to wave in a Palm Sunday procession.

- Divide the congregation into four groups to explore the feelings of different members of the crowd on Palm Sunday:

- the disciples;
- the cheering crowd;
- the Pharisees and teachers of the Law;
- Jesus.

Ask one person from each group to come forward and, using an interview method, explore the different feelings. This could lead into the talk or sermon.

- The whole congregation could be involved in a joyous procession. Children could wave brightly coloured streamers or large leaves. Choose songs to sing that are lively and easy to sing with easy-to-remember words. Remember this was a joyous procession in contrast to that of Good Friday. When the Pharisees told Jesus to quieten down the crowd, he replied that if they stopped singing the stones themselves would cry out. This could lead into the talk or sermon with an exploration on the change of emotions: Jesus weeping over the city, his anger in the Temple courtyard.

Prayers/ intercessions

(Based on Zechariah 9.9-12)

Leader   Rejoice, rejoice, people of Zion.

Shout for joy, you people of Jerusalem.

All   **Come Lord Jesus, we welcome you as our King.**

Leader   Look, your King is coming to you.

He comes triumphant and victorious but humble and riding on a donkey. (*Pause*)

Pray for those in authority that they may not abuse their power.

All   **Come Lord Jesus, we welcome you as our King.**

Leader   Your King will make peace among the nations. (*Pause*)

Pray for situations of war and conflict, that Christ may bring in his peace.

All   **Come Lord Jesus, we welcome you as our King.**

Leader   Your King will set people free. (*Pause*)

Pray for prisoners of conscience and places of oppression.

All   **Come Lord Jesus, we welcome you as our King.**

Leader   Your King will come with blessings to all who have suffered. (*Pause*)

Pray for those who are sick or suffering in any way.

All   **Come Lord Jesus, we welcome you as our King.**

Leader   Rejoice, rejoice, people of Zion.

Shout for joy, you people of Jerusalem.

Look, your King is coming to you.

All   **Come Lord Jesus, we welcome you as our King.**

Stories and other resources

Margaret Franks, *The Donkey's Tale,* Moorley's Print and Publishing, 1991

'Jesus on a donkey', in *Palm Tree Bible*, Palm Tree Press, 1992

'Palm Sunday', in *Pick and Mix* (p. 131)

'Palm Sunday', in *Festive Allsorts* (p. 24)

Drama

Ruth Tiller, 'God is working his purpose out', and 'A procession', in *Keeping the Feast*, Kevin Mayhew, 1995

Michael Forster, 'The donkey's day out', in *Act One*, Kevin Mayhew, 1996

Music

You are the King of Glory (SHF 630)

Hosanna, hosanna (song from Zimbabwe – WP 29)

You shall go out with joy (SHF 641)

King of kings and Lord of lords (SHF 305)

Halle, halle, halle (JU p. 80)

Hosanna, hosanna (HON 215)

Ride on, ride on in majesty! (HAMNS 61, HON 435, HTC 119)

At the name of Jesus (HAMNS 148, HON 46, HTC 172, SHF 26)

All glory, laud and honour (HAMNS 328, HON 11, HTC 120)

Post communion prayer

Lord Jesus Christ,
you humbled yourself in taking the form of a
    servant,
and in obedience died on the cross for our
    salvation:
give us the mind to follow you
and to proclaim you as Lord and King,
to the glory of God the Father.

Easter Day

 ## Readings

Isaiah 65.17-25

A vision of the 'new heaven and new earth' where all will have a healthy childhood and live to a ripe old age. There will be no need for weeping and none will be deprived of their home or their food. Perfect harmony.

or

Acts 10.34-43

Peter has made a significant step towards the Gentiles by responding to an invitation to visit Cornelius, a centurion. Peter addresses those gathered there, telling them how he witnessed the death and resurrection of Jesus and is now commanded to testify to everyone that Jesus is the one appointed by God and spoken of by the prophets.

1 Corinthians 15.19-26

Paul asserts his certainty about the resurrection. Just as it is certain that all descendants of Adam (all of us) will die, so it is certain that those of us in Christ are made alive. Paul describes the Second Coming of Christ and the final reign of God.

John 20.1-18

Mary Magdalene finds the tomb empty. She fetches Peter and John to come and see. When they have left she encounters the risen Jesus, mistaking him for the gardener but recognizing him when he calls her by name. Mary then goes to tell the others.

or

Luke 24.1-12

The women find the tomb empty and two angels tell them Jesus is risen. The women tell the disciples who do not believe them, but Peter runs to the tomb, finds the linen cloths and goes home amazed.

Collect

Lord of all life and power,
who through the mighty resurrection of your Son
overcame the old order of sin and death
to make all things new in him:
grant that we, being dead to sin
and alive to you in Jesus Christ,
may reign with him in glory;
to whom with you and the Holy Spirit
be praise and honour, glory and might,
now and in all eternity.

Talk/address/sermon

There is an old Russian Orthodox tradition of spending much of the day after Easter sitting around the table telling jokes. It was a way of imitating the cosmic joke that God enacted in the resurrection. Satan had begun to enjoy the feeling of winning, thinking he had had the last word, but then suddenly Jesus was risen, and life and salvation became the last words. So the whole world laughed at Satan's surprise defeat. A little research among the congregation will uncover suitable jokes with a surprise in the tail. (Heard the one about the fortunate character who slept right through the millennium in a coma? On awakening in the year 2020 he immediately rang his stockbroker who told him his shares in the water company were worth ten million pounds and his IBM shares worth fifteen million. 'I'm rich! I'm rich!' he shouted, until he was interrupted by the telephone operator saying, 'Your three minutes is up. Please insert one million pounds.')

Alternatively, take in a chocolate Easter egg, or other familiar 'resurrection' symbol (such as the crown, lamb, paschal candle or butterfly). Why do we use these symbols at Easter? How are they linked with the resurrection of Jesus? What is the 'new life' that he brings to us?

Congregational/ group activities

- Make an Easter Garden using soil and plants on a tray. Alternatively use a table and turn one side into a cave opening with cloth or cardboard and use a large stone for the seal. Decorate the tomb with potted plants.

- Make Easter biscuits using the following recipe – Ingredients for 20/25 biscuits: 6 oz butter, 8 oz caster sugar, 1 egg (beaten), 8 oz plain flour (sifted). Set oven to 175°C (350°F, gas mark 4)

  1. Cream butter and sugar.

  2. Add egg and flour.

  3. Mix into a dough.

  4. Shape as desired and put on greased trays.

  5. Cook on a middle shelf for about 20 minutes, or until golden.

  Ice the biscuits with shapes from the story such as Mary's tears in the garden, crosses on a hill, INRI, flowers in the garden, an open tomb, etc. Serve at coffee time or distribute to the congregation as they leave.

- Go back over the events of Holy Week. If the children were not involved in similar activities in Holy Week, break unleavened bread together, share a drink and wash a volunteer's feet.

- Give each person an A4 sheet of card. Fold these in half and draw a cross shape on one side. Cut out the shape and make a cross-shaped card.

Prayers/ intercessions

Distribute round stone-shaped pieces of card. Invite the congregation to write or draw their intercessions on the card and place it in or around the Easter Garden.

With a little more time and imagination, further reflection is possible by making a two-piece Easter prayer. This can be done by adding on a second card the new life or changed situation that God and the Easter people of the Church can bring to that situation. Fasten the two with a split pin and the new life (new heaven, new earth) will be revealed when the stone is rolled away.

Alternatively, use the prayers for Eastertide in *Lent, Holy Week, Easter* (pp. 277–82).

Stories and other resources

Eric Carle, *The Very Hungry Caterpillar*, H. Hamilton, 1994

Leslie Francis and Nicola Slee, *The Sunny Morning: Teddy Horsley Celebrates the New Life of Easter*, NCEC, 1989

'Jesus is alive!' (p. 67), and 'An Easter celebration' (p. 70), in *Praise, Play and Paint*

'The resurrection', in *Building New Bridges*

Drama

Dave Hopwood, 'Four Easter plays', in *A Fistful of Sketches*, NS/CHP, 1996

Derek Haylock, 'Garden path', in *Plays for All Seasons*, NS/CHP, 1997

Music

We'll sing a new song (SHF 582)

Easter tells us (BBP 41)

Happy Easter we will say (BBP 44)

I danced in the morning (HON 228)

Led like a lamb (HON 294, SHF 307)

Alleluia, alleluia, winter has fled (BBP 42)

This joyful Eastertide (HON 509, HTC 165)

Jesus Christ is ris'n today (HAMNS 77, HON 267, HTC 155, SHF 269)

Christ the Lord is ris'n again (HAMNS 79, HON 80, HTC 150)

Post communion prayer

God of Life,
who for our redemption gave your only-begotten
    Son to the death of the cross,
and by his glorious resurrection
have delivered us from the power of our enemy:
grant us so to die daily to sin,
that we may evermore live with him
    in the joy of his risen life;
through Jesus Christ our Lord.

Easter Day

The Second Sunday of Easter

 ## Readings

Exodus 14.10-31; 15.20-21*

This is the story of the crossing of the Red Sea by Moses and the Israelites and the destruction of Pharaoh's army.

* If the Old Testament reading is used on Sundays in Eastertide, the reading from Acts must be used as the second reading.

Acts 5.27-32

The apostles have been arrested, freed from jail by an angel and re-arrested while preaching again in the Temple. In this reading they appear before the Sanhedrin. The members of the high court are clearly worried that the apostles will try to avenge Jesus' death and have commanded them not to preach in Jesus' name. Peter tells the court that nothing can stop them from preaching about Jesus and about how God has given repentance and forgiveness to Israel through him.

Revelation 1.4-8

The great vision, revealed to John by an angel, begins with this greeting to the seven churches of Asia using a rich variety of biblical imagery describing God ('Alpha and Omega') and Jesus ('coming with the clouds') as it begins to describe 'what must soon take place' (verse 1).

John 20.19-31

The disciples gather in a locked room, fearful that the Jews who have killed Jesus may have something in store for them too. Then Jesus is among them, greeting them with the traditional Jewish greeting, now having added significance, 'Peace be with you.' First Jesus hands his mission on to the disciples and then, in language reminding us of God breathing life into Adam in Genesis 2, he fulfils the promise of the gift of the Spirit. Thomas, the 'doubter' or, more fairly, the 'realist', is not there and requires physical proof before he will believe. The following week he receives his proof when Jesus is with them again; John's Gospel reaches its climax as Thomas makes his declaration of faith.

Collect

Almighty Father,
you have given your only Son to die for our sins
and to rise again for our justification:
grant us so to put away the leaven of malice and
  wickedness
that we may always serve you
in pureness of living and truth;
through the merits of your Son Jesus Christ our
  Lord,
who is alive and reigns with you,
in the unity of the Holy Spirit,
one God, now and for ever.

Talk/address/ sermon

Sometimes, they say, you have to be a 'realist', but sometimes the 'idealist' approach is also respected. Draw up a list of some attitudes of the 'idealist' (such as 'all Third World debt should be cancelled', 'smoking/lottery/drinking should be banned'). Ask for contributions from the congregation. Draw up a comparative list of some of the attitudes of the 'realist' (such as 'the lottery provides money for charity and is an established part of life' or 'the governments won't agree on full Third World debt cancellation but might cut the debt level').

Some countries have very sophisticated medical procedures; others have none. The idealist might say you can't engage in transplants in rich countries until you can treat diarrhoea and measles in all countries. Would you like to be 'idealist' about 'medical fairness' or put it on the 'realist' list?

Was Thomas's response that of an 'idealist' or 'realist'? Can we sympathize with his attitude?

How had Jesus' physical body changed since his resurrection? Why was Thomas so ready to doubt what the other disciples told him? In what ways are we similar to Thomas – in only believing what we have seen for ourselves? What barriers do others put up to belief?

Congregational/ group activities

- Try some trust exercises. In pairs do some 'leading of the blind'. One partner is blindfolded and in silence the other leads them around the building, or even outside. Change roles and repeat. Afterwards discuss your feelings. How easy was it to trust your partner? What helped? What didn't? Select pairs  carefully and take precautions for this next exercise! Stand behind your partner without touching them and, when you are ready, ask them to fall backwards into your arms. It is easier to say than to do!

- Discuss in small groups: what barriers do people put up to faith? What reasons or excuses do they give for not believing in God, or for not coming to church? List these on a large sheet of paper. Then discuss ways that the Church could help to break down these barriers to belief.

 ## Prayers/ intercessions

Play some quiet instrumental music, light a candle and invite people silently to become aware (however dimly) of God's presence. Using a sand tray or bowl, give participants the opportunity to light a candle as a symbol of their own prayer for people or places that need to know the peace of God.

Use this thanksgiving prayer, which would be suitable for any Sunday service during Eastertide:

Our Lord Jesus Christ, risen from death, we praise you for changed lives and new hopes at Easter:

You came to Mary in the garden, and turned her tears into joy. For your love and your mercy:
we give you thanks, O Lord.

You came to the disciples in the upper room, and turned their fear into courage. For your love and your mercy:
we give you thanks, O Lord.

You came to the disciples by the lakeside, and turned their failure into faith. For your love and your mercy:
we give you thanks, O Lord.

You came to the disciples on the Emmaus road, and turned their despair into hope. For your love and your mercy:
we give you thanks, O Lord.

You come to us in our unworthiness and shame, and turn our weakness into triumph. For your love and your mercy:
we give you thanks, O Lord.

Lord Jesus, wherever there are tears, or fear, or failure, or despair, or weakness: come, reveal to us your love, your mercy, and your risen power; for the glory of your name. **Alleluia! Amen.**

Adapted from a prayer by Richard Hughes,
in *Church Family Worship* (no. 261)

 ## Stories and other resources

Susan Varley, *Badger's Parting Gift*, Collins, 1984

Leslie Francis and Nicola Slee, *The Windy Day: Teddy Horsley Learns About the Holy Spirit*, NCEC, 1989

Alan and Janet Ahlberg, *Burglar Bill*, Mammoth, 1989

Susan Sayers, 'Easter 1', in *Springboard to Worship*, Kevin Mayhew, 1989

Church Family Worship (no. 261)

'Understanding' (p. 164), in *Pick and Mix*

'Easter', in *Festive Allsorts* (p. 25)

Music

Peace be with you (WP 4)

Peace is flowing like a river (HON 412, SHF 431)

My peace I give unto you (SHF 377)

Domine Deus (JU p. 84)

Peace to you (HON 415)

Jesus, stand among us in thy risen pow'r (HON 280, HTC 364, SHF 291)

Thine be the glory (HAMNS 428, HON 503, HTC 167, SHF 545)

Peace, perfect peace (HON 413, HTC 467)

Post communion prayer

Lord God our Father,
through our Saviour Jesus Christ
you have assured your children of eternal life
and in baptism have made us one with him:
deliver us from the death of sin
and raise us to new life in your love,
in the fellowship of the Holy Spirit,
by the grace of our Lord Jesus Christ.

The Third Sunday of Easter

 ## Readings

Zephaniah 3.14-20

The Lord tells Zion to rejoice. He has overcome their enemies, he will gather his scattered people and will restore esteem and prosperity.

Acts 9.1-6[7-20]

Saul is on the road to Damascus with authorization to arrest any followers of 'The Way'. A vision blinds him and he hears a voice ask him why he is persecuting him. Then comes the great turning point in Saul's life as he asks the identity of the voice. Following this, he goes to the city to wait to hear what he should do. In verses 7-20, Ananias is told to accept Paul as a fellow disciple and to lay hands on him to restore his sight. After a few days with the disciples in Damascus, Paul begins to preach about Jesus.

Revelation 5.11-14

The writer uses his surreal artistry to describe Christ enthroned in heaven encircled and praised by the angels and all living things, singing 'Worthy is the Lamb' in a great vision of the Christian community's devotion to its Lord.

John 21.1-19

Jesus appears again to his disciples by the Sea of Tiberias. The stories and sayings in this second ending to John's Gospel are clearly laden with allegory. Most obvious perhaps are the centrality of the eucharistic meal with Jesus, which recalls the feeding of the 5,000 (6.11); the mission of the apostles to reach out to all sorts of 'fish' (the number may represent the belief that there were 153 species of fish: the fact that the net does not break, despite the number and variety of fish, indicates the capacity of the Church to contain people of all sorts and needs).

Peter is carefully and lovingly reinstated by Jesus, given opportunity to declare his love three times, just as he denied it three times. This is probably written after Peter had suffered, but his future role as pastor and martyr is foretold.

Collect

Almighty Father,
who in your great mercy gladdened the disciples
    with the sight of the risen Lord:
give us such knowledge of his presence with us,
that we may be strengthened and sustained
    by his risen life
and serve you continually in righteousness and
    truth;
through Jesus Christ your Son our Lord,
who is alive and reigns with you,
in the unity of the Holy Spirit,
one God, now and for ever.

 ## Talk/address/ sermon

God becomes real for us in many ways. Invite contributions, either prepared beforehand or spontaneously, from individuals prepared to describe times when God's presence is real. Without such times it is difficult to sustain belief, but we need to put aside times of 'prayer' or 'meditation' for it to happen. The power of the resurrection is that so many have 'known' the risen Christ, by taking time to do these ordinary things: go to the tomb, listen to the gardener, have breakfast on the shore or talk to strangers on the road.

 ## Congregational/ group activities

- Reinforce the story of the 'miraculous catch' with an 'Into the Net' game. Cut out paper fish, place or draw a net on the floor and see how quickly you can encourage all the fish along the floor and into the net by wafting (not touching) the fish along with magazines or newspapers. The game is also known as 'Flip the Kipper'.

- Do a little research on different species of fish, size, shape, habitat and lifestyle, and bring pictures, slides or video clips to show. Invite everyone to consider whether they see anything of themselves in the descriptions. Work on this together or in pairs. You may need to invent some new fish. Help each person to draw and cut out the shape of their fish, adding words or colour if time allows, and display them on a board or collage.

- Share a breakfast together. Even if barbecued fish is too difficult to prepare, use pictures and/or your imagination to put yourself onto the lakeside with the disciples and discuss what you might want to ask or tell Jesus.

Prayers/ intercessions

Write or draw on paper fishes the people, places or concerns that need to be drawn into God's net of love and care. At the end of the prayers or the service ask everyone to take out one concern and carry it with them into the wider ocean of God's love by remembering it in their personal prayers during the week.

Give out loaf-shaped cards in a variety of colours and, in silence or to some reflective music, give time for everyone to call to mind things, places or people which have opened their eyes to the reality of God with them. Write or draw on the cards as an act of thanksgiving. Collect the cards and display them as a reminder of the many ways God may be made known to all of us.

Stories and other resources

Susan Sayers, 'Easter 1', in *Springboard to Worship*, Kevin Mayhew, 1989

The material from 'The Conversion of St Paul', in *Seasons, Saints and Sticky Tape* (p. 18)

 ## Music

From hand to hand (BBP 55)

Peter and James and John in a sailboat (JP 197)

I am the bread of life (SHF 182)

James and Andrew, Peter and John (HON 257)

This is his body (SHF 546)

Jesus stand among us (SHF 290)

Lord, enthroned in heav'nly splendour (HAMNS 263, HON 309)

Bread of heav'n, on thee we feed (HAMNS 271, HON 67)

Alleluia, sing to Jesus (HAMNS 262, HON 26, HTC 170)

Post communion prayer

Living God,
your Son made himself known to his disciples
in the breaking of bread:
open the eyes of our faith,
that we may see him in all his redeeming work;
who is alive and reigns, now and for ever.

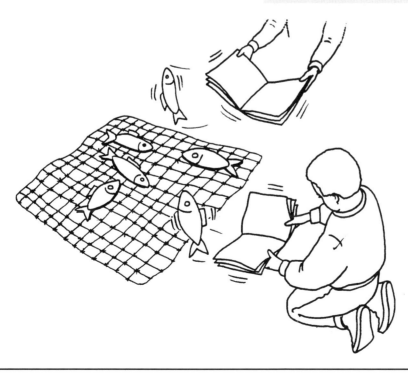

The Fourth Sunday of Easter

Readings

Genesis 7.1-5,11-18; 8.6-18; 9.8-13

These interspersed readings follow the well–known story of Noah: from God's call to Noah to build an ark, through the flood, to the sign of the rainbow as God's renewed covenant.

Acts 9.36-43

Peter brings Tabitha (Dorcas) back to life, reminding us of Elijah and the widow's son and Jesus and Jairus's daughter. She had done much good in her life, given to those in need and made clothes for the widows, who would have received special support from the Christian community.

Revelation 7.9-17

A great crowd surrounds the throne of 'the Lamb' giving perfect praise. They wear white robes because they have been through 'the great tribulation' (perhaps John's church was going through a particularly difficult time). God will protect them, and 'the Lamb' will be their shepherd.

John 10.22-30

Some hostile Jews accuse Jesus of failing to make a straightforward statement about whether he is the Messiah. In one sense it is true, only the Samaritan woman at the well has heard Jesus describe himself as Messiah. But, on the other hand, what he has done and the things he has said have made it perfectly clear to those ready to hear (his sheep). Those who are Jesus' sheep listen to him, recognize him and follow him.

Collect

Almighty God,
whose Son Jesus Christ is the resurrection and
    the life:
raise us, who trust in him,
from the death of sin to the life of righteousness,
that we may seek those things which are above,
where he reigns with you
in the unity of the Holy Spirit,
one God, now and for ever.

Talk/address/ sermon

Use the shepherd and sheep collage, produced during the congregational/ group activities as a visual aid for this talk.

Do you want to be thought of as a sheep? There are many unattractive aspects to this image that is used by Jesus in today's Gospel reading. However, it is universally true that human beings orientate their lives in a particular direction by referring to a set of values,  which religious people call a faith. Sometimes people consciously think about these values, other times they are subconscious guides to our behaviour. Jesus laid down his life to make the way clear to us; we can recognize his voice and put our values and behaviour alongside his if we choose. He is the great Shepherd, who has given us values to live by and a voice to follow – if we are willing to be his sheep.

Congregational/ group activities

- Make a collage of the shepherd with the sheep. Talk about the qualities you would like in the person responsible for leading you and caring for you. Write these on pieces of paper and stick them on or around the shepherd. Ask everyone to cut out a sheep, put their name on it and stick it on the collage. If there is time, add some more sheep to your local flock or think about the worldwide flock and include representatives from other countries.

- Give each group five sheets of paper. Ask each group either to make a list or draw pictures to be used during the intercessions. The lists should cover the prayer requests on the themes:

  - the Church;
  - home;
  - work (weekday activities or school);
  - the world (work for peace and justice).

Prayers/ intercessions

Pray facing the four corners of the church in turn, representing the commitment to follow Jesus in all aspects of our lives. Put the pictures or prayers produced by the groups in each corner and ask someone to lead a prayer. The corners would represent the church, home, weekday activity/work/school, the world/work for peace and justice.

Stories and other resources

'The lost sheep', *Palm Tree Bible*, Palm Tree Press, 1992

Taffy Davies, *Miles and the Screwdriver*, Scripture Union, 1985

The *Following Jesus* series, Bible Reading Fellowship

Drama

Dave Hopwood, 'The gospel truth', *Acting Up*, NS/CHP, 1995

Music

Wherever you go, I will follow (BBP 16)

One more step along the world I go (HON 405)

Worthy is the lamb (SHF 621)

There's a sound on the wind (SHF 540)

The Lord, the Lord, the Lord is my shepherd (BBP 19)

The God of love my shepherd is (HAMNS 110, HON 479)

Loving Shepherd of thy sheep (HAMNS 134, HON 325, HTC 305)

The King of love my shepherd is (HAMNS 126, HON 484, HTC 44, SHF 513)

Post communion prayer

Merciful Father,
you gave your Son Jesus Christ to be the good shepherd,
and in his love for us to lay down his life and rise again:
keep us always under his protection,
and give us grace to follow in his steps;
through Jesus Christ our Lord.

The Fifth Sunday of Easter

 ## Readings

Baruch 3.9-15,32 – 4.4

Israel is told that obeying God leads to peace and prosperity. Through wisdom the people will come to know what pleases God.

or

Genesis 22.1-18

This is the story of Abraham and the near–sacrifice of Isaac.

Acts 11.1-18

Peter returns to Jerusalem after his visit to Cornelius (one of the possible readings for Easter Day). He is in trouble with the Jewish Christians for eating with non-Jews, as this makes him ritually unclean. Jewish Christians saw Jesus as the Jewish Messiah, and a Gentile wanting to become a follower of 'The Way' would first have to obey the Jewish Law. Peter recounts the story of his dream and the way the Spirit came to the people in Cornelius's house, just as it did to the apostles at Pentecost. God clearly intends the message to be for everyone.

Revelation 21.1-6

All evil has been destroyed and the sea, traditionally seen as a devouring monster, is no more. A new heaven and a new earth are created. Jerusalem, the holy city, is transformed and made new. God makes his home among human beings; death, mourning and pain are no more. God is making all things new.

John 13.31-35

This passage follows the washing of the disciples' feet and the departure of Judas. Jesus' Passion and glori-fication has been anticipated in the foot–washing. He now tells the disciples that he will be with them for only a short while more. Jesus leaves the followers one command: to love one another. It is by this mutual love that they will be recognized as disciples, and so it is to be a distinguishing mark.

Collect

Almighty God,
who through your only-begotten Son Jesus Christ
have overcome death and opened to us
    the gate of everlasting life:
grant that, as by your grace going before us
    you put into our minds good desires,
so by your continual help
we may bring them to good effect;
through Jesus Christ our risen Lord,
who is alive and reigns with you,
in the unity of the Holy Spirit,
one God, now and for ever.

 ## Talk/address/ sermon

Peter's visit to Cornelius made him change the way he looked at the world. Earlier his dream had challenged him to revise his view of what was acceptable to eat. His shock might be compared to that some of us might feel if God told us to start using the words we regard as swear-words or to wear outlandish clothes. God constantly calls us to review things and change, but it is a call that is not too diffi-cult to ignore, especially in a comfortable, settled society. So who is your Cornelius? What or who is ask-ing you to think again, to consider change?

Congregational/ group activities

- Identify as many signs of people loving one another as you can, noting them quickly on a large sheet of paper. Now put a circle round the signs of love that members of your church show to one another. If you like, put a square round the ones that are to be seen in your church's relationships with other churches in the area. Finally, mark the ones that are visible in your relationships with Christians on other continents.

- Role–play, 'What am I doing?' Write down on separate file cards, or small pieces of paper, the words 'Love is . . .' followed by an appropriate saying (such as 'washing up', 'helping someone to do their homework', 'comforting someone when they are sad'). Give a card to each person in the group and ask them in turn to mime the saying. Can the others guess what they are doing? Ask the group to make up their own sayings to act out.

Prayers/intercessions

Use the following prayer from the Iona Community to think of ways that God is challenging us to change: in our attitude to others and in the way that we live.

New Ways

God of our lives
you are always calling us
to follow you into the future,
inviting us to new ventures, new challenges,
new ways to care,
new ways to touch the hearts of all.
When we are fearful of the unknown, give us courage.
When we worry that we are not up to the task,
remind us that you would not call us
if you did not believe in us.

When we get tired,
or feel disappointed with the way things are going,
remind us that you can bring change and hope
out of the most difficult situations.

Kathy Galloway, in *The Pattern of Our Days*
(no. 47, p. 142)

Stories and other resources

David McKee, *Tusk Tusk,* Red Fox, 1983

'Love', in *Pick and Mix* (p. 112)

The Pattern of Our Days (no. 47)

Music

Make me a channel of your peace (HON 328)

I am the church (JU p. 24)

A new commandment I give unto you (HON 4, SHF 14)

Love is his word, love is his way (HON 322)

You are the vine (SHF 633)

Love divine, all loves excelling (HAMNS 131, HON 321, HTC 217, SHF 353)

When I needed a neighbour (HAMNS 433, HON 548)

Help us to help each other, Lord (HAMNS 374, HON 208, HTC 540)

Post communion prayer

Eternal God,
whose Son Jesus Christ is the way, the truth, and the life:
grant us to walk in his way,
to rejoice in his truth,
and to share his risen life;
who is alive and reigns, now and for ever.

The Sixth Sunday of Easter

Readings

Ezekiel 37.1-14

The prophet is shown a valley full of dry bones. The prophet speaks the words of the Lord to the bones and they take form and come alive. The house of Israel is compared to the dry bones: their hope gone. Yet the Lord promises to raise them up, revive them and resettle them in their own land.

Acts 16.9-15

This is the beginning of the passages in Acts which use the pronoun 'we', presumably showing that Luke has now joined the group. There were few Jews in Philippi and no synagogue, just a gathering place in the open air by the river. Lydia understands quite clearly what Paul is saying and so she is baptized. Consequently her household is baptized with her.

Revelation 21.10,22 – 22.5

Here are more of the delights of the New Jerusalem. This might be seen as a view of the Church exercising its mission to the world, bringing light and healing to the nations and their leaders, making clear the shining presence of God and containing streams of refreshingly pure water.

John 14.23-29

Jesus shares with the disciples a picture of the circle of love and obedience which runs between them, himself and the Father. The Paraclete, the Holy Spirit, is described here as the one who will help the disciples apply what they have heard. The disciples are encouraged not to be sad or fearful when Jesus is no longer with them, but to be happy that he is with the Father.

or

John 5.1-9

When Jesus goes to the pool of Bethesda in Jerusalem he sees an invalid lying nearby. Jesus heals him. As this happened on the Sabbath, many of the Jews take offence at his actions and seek to persecute him.

Collect

God our redeemer,
you have delivered us from the power of darkness
and brought us into the kingdom of your Son:
grant, that as by his death he has recalled us to
    life,
so by his continual presence in us he may raise
    us to eternal joy;
through Jesus Christ your Son our Lord,
who is alive and reigns with you,
in the unity of the Holy Spirit,
one God, now and for ever.

Talk/address/ sermon

Jesus has been living and talking with the disciples for a long time now. They have begun to understand and come to terms with some of the things he has been saying. They have grown to enjoy this lifestyle, mostly. But now all is to change: the certainties, the understandings are undermined as Jesus talks about leaving them. The disciples are challenged to think about a new role, not travelling and talking with Jesus but continuing with the help of the Paraclete, Comforter, Counsellor. Death may be a useful parallel for us. Members of the congregation may be reminded of helpful insights from their own bereavements. *Badger's Parting Gift* or *Mudge, Gill and Steve* might be useful stories to tell.

Congregational/ group activities

- Using clay or a similar modelling material, create a representation of the Paraclete joining Jesus, God and yourself. It might turn out as a key ring linking keys, an Olympic-style symbol or one of those puzzles you try (and usually fail) to take apart.

- Make one of the trees of life (described in the Revelation passage), or use a budding branch and add on colourful paper leaves with words or pictures of things which might bring healing to the nations. You could think of actions, values or insights which would build heavenly communities out of our own nation and other difficult places round the world.

Prayers/ intercessions

Pray for:

- those who have loved you in the past;
- those who have helped your faith;
- those who laugh with you;
- those who pray for you.

Make paper chains with a link for yourself and one for each of the people you have just thought of. Leave the chain available for others to add their prayers later.

Use this prayer from *Patterns for Worship* which takes up the theme of resurrection:

We pray to Jesus who is present with us to eternity,
    saying,
Jesus, Lord of life:
in your mercy, hear us.

Jesus, light of the world,
bring the light and peace of your gospel
to the nations . . .
Jesus, Lord of life:
in your mercy, hear us.

Jesus, bread of life,
give food to the hungry . . .
and nourish us all with your word.
Jesus, Lord of life:
in your mercy, hear us.

Jesus, our way, our truth, our life,
be with us and all who follow you in the way . . .
deepen our appreciation of your truth,
and fill us with your life.
Jesus, Lord of life:
in your mercy, hear us.

Jesus, Good Shepherd who gave your life for the
    sheep,
recover the straggler, bind up the injured,
strengthen the sick
and lead the healthy and strong to play.
Jesus, Lord of life:
in your mercy, hear us.
Jesus, the resurrection and the life,
we give you thanks
for all who have lived and believed in you . . .
raise us with them to eternal life.
Jesus, Lord of life:
in your mercy, hear us,
accept our prayers, and be with us always. Amen.

Patterns for Worship (pp. 72–3)

Stories and other resources

Susan Varley, *Badger's Parting Gift*, Collins, 1984

Doris Stickney, *Waterbugs and Dragonflies*, Mowbray, 1997

Jim Dainty, *Mudge, Gill and Steve*, NS/CHP, 1997

Patterns for Worship (pp. 72–3)

 ## Music

Don't be afraid (CAYP p. 72)

Nade te turbe (Taizé song – HON 347)

My peace I give unto you (SHF 377)

God has put a circle round us (BBP 46)

The love of God (JU p. 86)

This is my body, broken for you (HON 506)

Come, thou Holy Spirit, come (HAMNS 92, HON 97)

O King enthroned on high (HAMNS 158, HON 373)

May the grace of Christ our Saviour (HAMNS 181, HON 333, HTC 370)

Post communion prayer

God our Father,
    whose Son Jesus Christ gives the water of eternal
        life:
    may we thirst for you,
    the spring of life and source of goodness,
    through him who is alive and reigns, now and for
        ever.

The Seventh Sunday of Easter

Sunday after Ascension Day

 ## Readings

Ezekiel 36.24-28

The Lord tells the Israelites he will take them, cleanse them and give them a new spirit. They will keep his laws and live in the God-given land of their ancestors.

Acts 16.16-34

The story of Paul and Silas, who having been arrested for healing a girl possessed by a devil, are imprisoned. An earthquake opens the doors and loosens their chains but they choose not to escape. The grateful jailer tends to their wounds, is baptized and takes them up to his house for a meal.

Revelation 22.12-14,16,17,20,21

This is the very last part of the book of Revelation and looks forward to the Second Coming, mentioning Alpha and Omega.

John 17.20-26

This is the part of the Last Supper prayer, before Jesus and his disciples leave for the garden of Gethsemane. Jesus prays to God for all who put their trust in him. He also prays that we may be as one, as Jesus and God are one, and that the name of God may be known.

Collect

O God the King of glory,
you have exalted your only Son Jesus Christ
with great triumph to your kingdom in heaven:
we beseech you, leave us not comfortless,
but send your Holy Spirit to strengthen us
and exalt us to the place
    where our Saviour Christ is gone before,
who is alive and reigns with you,
in the unity of the Holy Spirit,
one God, now and for ever.

 ## Talk/address/sermon

Have a selection of recent newspaper headings available, showing a mixture of 'good' and 'bad' news. What is 'good news'? Who should do it? How do we share it? Is it best shown through words or action? *Discuss the story from Acts and other examples of unjust imprisonment.* What can imprison us today? Unjust social structures, poverty, ignorance, or addiction? What sets us free? How do we free others? Are chains always bad? What of a ship's anchors or the bonds of love and friendship?

 ## Congregational/group activities

- Explore activities of charities committed to breaking bonds of oppression, addiction or poverty, such as Amnesty International or Christian Aid.

- Make visual aids for Pentecost such as tongues of fire mitres or a collage for an altar frontal.

- Prepare for next week's Pentecost service by thinking about how we absorb information through our five senses both unconsciously and deliberately. Why are fire and mighty winds such powerful messengers? How do we experience them through each of the senses? How can we demonstrate them? What do we learn of God?

- In small groups make paper chains of all the things that imprison or restrict us from being the people God created us to be. Use the chains to bar the way to God's presence in word or sacrament. Explore how that feels. Break the chains in an appropriate symbolic way so that all the congregation can pass through. Explore how that freedom and reconciliation feels. At the Peace re-tie the bonds that bind us together in the love of Christ.

- Identify the good things that the Holy Spirit can bring. Give all the congregation a pen and piece of paper to write these down. The written responses could be mounted on a mobile, or placed on fruit (of the Spirit) templates.

- Compose a congregational 'mission statement'. What would we want to share with others about our group, faith or church, i.e. what is good about our church?

Prayers/ intercessions

Obtain slides from Tear Fund or Amnesty International depicting those in prison or whose lives are blighted by injustice, ignorance or addiction. Pray through the top-ioo outlined below.

Thanksgiving: for the love of God that sets us free;

for our freedom to worship;

for those who brought the gospel to us;

for all those who work to set others free.

Intercession: for those who are persecuted and imprisoned for their faith;

for those who have yet to hear or respond to the gospel;

for ourselves that we might be freed from the sins that bind us;

for courage to speak out against oppression;

for all those whose lives are blighted by injustice or addiction.

Use the response:

Leader   God of all the world

All   **hear our prayers today.**

Stories and other resources

Leslie Francis and Nicola Slee, *The Windy Day: Teddy Horsley Learns About the Holy Spirit*, NCEC, 1987

Missionary stories, *Festive Allsorts* (St Aidan, p. 48; St Columba, p. 36)

'Holy Spirit' (p. 81), 'Gifts' (p. 68) and 'Stewardship' (p. 151), in *Pick and Mix*

 ## Music

Father make us one (SHF 95)

As we are gathered, Jesus is here (HON 40, SHF 24)

Bind us together (SHF 39)

Open our eyes, Lord (SHF 420)

Veni Sancte Spiritus (MT1 p. 36)

Forth in the peace of Christ we go (HAMNS 458, HON 142, HTC 542)

Eternal Father, strong to save (HAMNS 292, HON 114, HTC 285)

Holy Spirit, truth divine (HTC 235)

Post communion prayer

Eternal God, giver of love and power,
your Son Jesus Christ has sent us into all the world
to preach the gospel of his kingdom:
confirm us in this mission,
and help us to live the good news we proclaim;
through Jesus Christ our Lord.

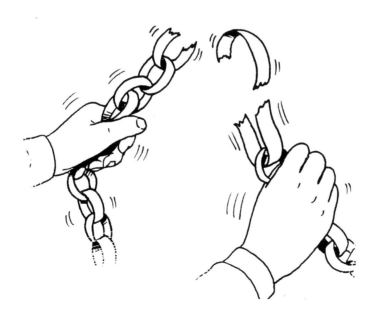

Day of Pentecost

Whit Sunday

 ## Readings

Acts 2.1-21

The Holy Spirit comes with power upon the disciples. The crowd in Jerusalem, from 'every nation under heaven' can hear and understand the good news of God's saving power. Peter, with the eleven, lifts up his voice and speaks above the babel of tongues, choosing the prophet Joel as his starting point.

Genesis 11.1-9

The skyscraper of Babel shows man at his most arrogant, defiantly reaching up to the heavens to show his great achievements. The unity of languages and a common intention bring great possibilities for both good and evil – either to make a name for ourselves or to live humbly under God.

John 14.8-17[25-27]

Philip fails to realize that to have seen Jesus is to have seen God the Father in human form. Those who believe in Christ belong to God even as Christ is God: to love is to obey. Just as God dwells in human form in Christ so will the Spirit of God dwell within each person who belongs to Christ.

Romans 8.14-17

In this brief passage, Paul explains how Christ's sacrifice has brought us into a new relationship with God. We are not only children of God, able to call him 'Abba, Father!' but also joint heirs with Christ in both his suffering and glory.

Collect

> God, who as at this time
> taught the hearts of your faithful people
> by sending to them the light of your Holy Spirit:
> grant us by the same Spirit
> to have a right judgement in all things
> and evermore to rejoice in his holy comfort;
> through the merits of Christ Jesus our Saviour,
> who is alive and reigns with you,
> in the unity of the Holy Spirit,
> one God, now and for ever.

 ## Talk/address/ sermon

This visual aid needs considerable preparation before the service begins. Due caution should be taken in the handling of the methylated spirits and the use of the aid. Small aperture wire netting is put in the base of a biscuit tin which is then filled with sand to a depth of about 50 mm so that it is level with the top of the tin. A candle is hidden in the sand so that only its wick is showing. The congregation are asked if it is possible to set light to this dead, inert mass of sand. (Offer if necessary the opportunity to demonstrate!) Explain that what is missing is the spirit. However, you've brought some with you; reveal the methylated spirits bottle. Caution everyone about the dangers of flames but then pour spirit over the sand and set alight with a taper. The blue flames will dance over the surface of the sand in a very evocative way, sometimes focused in one area only to die away and spring up dramatically in another. When they finally fade away the hidden candle is left alight by the spirit with all the opportunities to draw the theological comparisons.

 ## Congregational/ group activities

- Make simple paper or other aerial sailing boats and race on the local boating lake or stream.

- Make musical instruments of the wind variety from scrap materials.

- Make a colourful windsock and hang from church tower or give to local primary school.

- Design and make vestments/frontal banner/hangings for worship areas depicting wind and fire.

- Build Lego towers in small groups to demonstrate how much effort, co-operation and determination is required to build a tower to reach the skies; and how great is the human desire to put ourselves in God's place. Notice how easily competition creeps in between the groups. Reflect upon all that could be achieved through God's grace if that energy were directed towards God's will being done on earth as it is in heaven.

- Play a variation of Chinese Whispers to explore the value of everyone hearing the same message. It also shows the care required to remember and faithfully pass on the life-giving message entrusted to us, and the need to check out that the message received is the message intended.

- The energetic might like to practise a liturgical dance involving all the congregation. Some should stand in groups or singly, while other members of the congregation weave and wend their way in and around them carrying long 'flame' streamers. An appropriate song on the work of the Holy Spirit (such as those listed below) might be used to accompany the dance.

 ## Prayers/ intercessions

Use the following response during the time of intercession:

> We pray for love, the gift of the Spirit,
> that we might show love to . . .
> **Come, Holy Spirit, live in us.**
>
> We pray for joy, the gift of the Spirit,
> that we might bring joy to . . .
> **Come, Holy Spirit, live in us.**
>
> We pray for peace, the gift of the Spirit,
> that we might bring peace to . . .
> **Come, Holy Spirit, live in us.**
>
> We pray for patience/kindness, etc.,
> the gift of the Spirit, that we might . . .
> **Come, Holy Spirit, live in us.**

 ## Stories and other resources

'Holy Spirit', in *Pick and Mix* (p. 81)

'Pentecost', in *Seasons, Saints and Sticky Tape* (p. 40)

 ## Drama

Derek Haylock, 'That's the spirit', in *Plays for All Seasons*, NS/CHP, 1997

Dave Hopwood, 'Pentecost rap', in *A Fistful of Sketches*, NS/CHP, 1996

Ruth Tiller, 'The fiery furnace', in *Keeping the Feast*, Kevin Mayhew, 1995

Music

All over the world the Spirit is moving (HON 16)

Colours of day dawn into the mind (HON 87)

It's the presence of your Spirit, Lord, we need (SHF 236)

Ask and it shall be given (SHF 20)

Come, O Holy Spirit, come (WP 79)

Come down, O love divine (HAMNS 156, HON 90, HTC 231)

Come, Holy Ghost, our souls inspire (HAMNS 493, HON 92, HTC 589)

Breathe on me, breath of God (HAMNS 157, HON 69, HTC 226, SHF 47)

Post communion prayer

Faithful God,
who fulfilled the promises of Easter
by sending us your Holy Spirit
and opening to every race and nation
the way of life eternal:
open our lips by your Spirit,
that every tongue may tell of your glory;
through Jesus Christ our Lord.

Trinity Sunday

 ## Readings

Proverbs 8.1-4,22-31

In this passage from Proverbs, wisdom and understanding are equated and personified. The first act of God is to create Wisdom who was before all and in all that he created after her. She calls out to humanity to hear her voice.

Romans 5.1-5

To the church at Rome Paul writes of peace and grace, hope and glory, because of reconciliation with God through Jesus Christ. He speaks too of God pouring love into the hearts of all who have received the gift of the Holy Spirit.

John 16.12-15

Christ tells his disciples that the truth is revealed to them as they are able to receive it. They must be guided into all truth by the Holy Spirit when he comes. Christ clearly links together the work of the Trinity – the Father, Son and Spirit in unity in their revelation of God to mankind.

Collect

Almighty and everlasting God,
you have given us your servants grace,
by the confession of a true faith,
to acknowledge the glory of the eternal Trinity
and in the power of the divine majesty to worship
   the Unity:
keep us steadfast in this faith,
that we may evermore be defended from all adversities;
through Jesus Christ your Son our Lord,
who is alive and reigns with you,
in the unity of the Holy Spirit,
one God, now and for ever.

 ## Talk/address/ sermon

Sometimes our experience and intuition reveal truths to us that defy explanation or cold logic. For example, we know from experience that although a stopped clock is logically more useful than one in error by a few seconds a day, in practice this is not true. The Christian community experiences God as Trinity: Father, Son and Holy Spirit, one God in three Persons. Theologians have struggled for centuries to explain the Trinity. The following illustration is another attempt to explain it.

Make a visual aid from a strip of a single thin card about 80 mm wide by 900 mm long. Draw lines along its length to divide into three and write 'Father', 'Son', 'Holy Spirit' in different sectors. Join the ends of the card to make a ring that speaks of God as unending love. The card is still one card and the persons of the Trinity are not distinctly separate, so this is not yet an adequate model. If we were to cut the strip into three we would have three separate persons but they would be unconnected – three gods, not the one God we know. But there's a twist to the story. God the Father reveals himself as the Son, so let's put a 90 degree twist in our card and re-join the ends. In fact we need two twists because Jesus also promises that the Spirit will come.

Our one card now is a circle with two twists with the lines that indicate the persons of the Trinity meeting together on the outside. If the one card is now cut along the lines to divide it into three pieces the result will be three rings, each of which is interlocked and inseparable from two others. One card, in three pieces, still one entity from the original card.

 ## Congregational/ group activities

- Think of all the ways that Christians have tried to explain the doctrine of the Trinity, such as the clover leaf, triangle, interwoven rings, three-in-one oil, the three forms of water – ice, water and steam. Make a collage or a series of banners using these symbols.

- Use the Rublev Icon of the Trinity as a starting point to think about God, Father/Son/Holy Spirit and as Creator/Saviour/Life-giver. How is the Trinity portrayed? What does the Icon tell us of the relationship among the Trinity? Design and paint an icon for personal use.

- Traditional explanations or models of the Trinity are usually verbal or visual. We are creations gifted with other senses – hearing, smell, touch and taste. Find ways to show how these gifts can be used to give expression to our understanding of God as Trinity, e.g. through music or cooking.

- In small groups make a list of all the words and pictures that have been used to talk about our God – who is the mystery beyond our wildest imaginings but who reveals himself to us his creatures that we might have a relationship of love with him. Share those lists with the other groups. Pick some of the words that are especially helpful and write them on banners in large pictures or letters.

Prayers/intercessions

Link the prayers around the following Trinitarian themes:

Prayers to the Father who watches over his creation with a mother's love, including thanksgiving for the wonder of the universe and its awesome intimacy; acknowledgement of our ecological failures and social injustices.

Prayers to the Saviour Son who shared our life and showed us how to be human; for everything in our personal and communal life that needs to be transformed through forgiveness and sacrifice.

Prayers to the Holy Spirit of God who lives in us and translates our feeblest approaches to love into songs of worship and action; for the wisdom of God that surpasses all understanding; for courage and insight to live holy lives.

Prayers to the Holy Trinity, the one who is three, and the three who are one; that as God is love in community we too might live through grace and be communities of living love.

Stories and other resources

David Adam, *Meditations on the Hymn of St Patrick*, Triangle, 1987

Martin Wallace, *Pocket Celtic Prayers*, NS/CHP, 1996

'St Patrick', in *Seasons, Saints and Sticky Tape* (p. 28)

'God', in *Pick and Mix* (p. 73)

'Trinity', in *Festive Allsorts* (p. 34)

 # Music

We believe in God the Father (HON 530)

Be still, for the presence of the Lord (HON 53)

Father, we adore you (HON 125, SHF 96)

Father, we love you (HON 126, SHF 98)

Glory to God (Peruvian Gloria – JU p. 78)

Laudate Dominum (HON 291, MT1 p. 10)

I bind unto myself today (HON 225, HTC 5)

Holy, holy, holy! Lord God almighty! (HAMNS 95, HON 212, HTC 7, SHF 168)

Be thou my vision (HAMNS 343, HON 56, HTC 545, SHF 38)

Post communion prayer

Almighty and eternal God,
you have revealed yourself as Father, Son and
Holy Spirit,
and live and reign in the perfect unity of love:
hold us firm in this faith,
that we may know you in all your ways
and evermore rejoice in your eternal glory,
who are three Persons yet one God,
now and for ever.

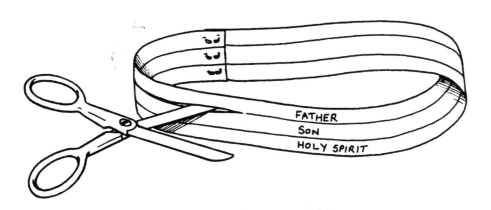

Trinity Sunday

Sunday between 29 May and 4 June

(if after Trinity Sunday)

Proper 4

 ### Readings

Continuous

1 Kings 18.20,21[22-29]30-39

Elijah's challenge to the people of Israel is simple and stark – choose God or Baal. His courageous challenge to the prophets of Baal is equally forthright – put your god to the test against the one true God. On this mountain of Carmel the followers of Baal find only silence and failure but the God of Elijah answers his prophet's prayer. The fire of the Lord consumes all and the people of Israel return to their God.

or Related

1 Kings 8.22,23,41-43

King Solomon, man of wisdom and of prayer, is also a man of vision and hope. This prayer of dedication of the house he has built to honour the God of Israel is that all peoples of the earth, not just the present Israel, should come to this house to acknowledge and worship the God of all peoples.

Galatians 1.1-12

Paul, called by the grace of God to be an apostle, writes urgently and fiercely to the church in Galatia calling them back to the gospel of Christ. He refutes the idea that he is trying to win people's approval for himself, or that he made up the message. The gospel message is not man-made, but received by revelation from Jesus Christ.

Luke 7.1-10

A centurion, a man of authority, recognizes an authority far greater than his own and as a result his sick servant is healed. His faith causes the Saviour of the world to marvel that nowhere in Israel has he found such faith – not even in his home town.

 ### Talk/address/ sermon

The readings all centre on authority, leadership and faith. Elijah on Mount Carmel is full of courage, confronting and challenging the forces of evil. Solomon at this point in his leadership provides a focus of Israel's worship and a vision for the Gentiles. Paul, a Jewish Christian, exerts his influence and authority on the Gentile Galatians in order that they might return to the true faith. These stories come to focus in the Gospel reading and are turned on their head. The Gentile centurion now justifies Solomon's hope and impresses Christ from a distance by his faith found nowhere in all Israel. So by what authority do *we* live and in whose name do we act? How does our own faith stand up in comparison to that of the Gentile centurion?

 ### Congregational/ group activities

- Find someone who served in the armed forces ranks during a time of conflict and someone else whose role involved giving orders. Ask them to tell the group their stories and impressions of that time. Explore with each other the different ways leadership is experienced – the children will have insights too! Where does authority come from? What are the qualities of a true leader?

- Divide the group into two teams and play a game such as Connect 4 or Snakes and Ladders (or other games that can be played in teams). Who undertakes what role in each team and how is that decided? Who decides which piece should be moved (or who throws the dice)? Do the roles change during the course of the game? How is leadership exercised, how are decisions made and who has authority?

- Ask members of the congregation to choose from a pile of hats one which appeals to them. The pile can include helmets and caps from the police/fire service/armed forces as well as civilian toppers, cloth caps, miners/site helmets, etc. As many people as are willing should say why they have chosen their hat and what sort of person they think would wear it. Discuss whether or not people are defined by their roles and fit into neat categories. Relate to church life and faith journey.

Prayers/intercessions

Focus the prayers on those in authority and pray for the following:

- for courage and integrity in preaching the gospel;
- for Church leaders and the leaders of other faiths;
- for the leaders of the nations and those in authority;
- for police officers and members of the armed forces, especially their chaplains;
- for magistrates, judges and all who work in the courts of law;
- for prison officers, chaplains and members of the probation service;
- for teachers, lecturers and school governors.

Leader   Lord, give them courage and faith

All   **to speak your word of truth.**

Stories and other resources

Philip Welsh, 'Harvey the skateboarding octopus', in *The Reluctant Mole and Other Beastly Tales,* Scripture Union, 1979

'St Oswald', in *Festive Allsorts* (p. 45)

Music

Father, I place into your hands (HON 121, SHF 94)

Meekness and majesty (HON 335)

He is Lord, he is Lord (HON 204, SHF 159)

I love you Lord Jesus (BBP 27)

Praise God from whom all blessings flow (SHF 436)

Ye servants of God (HON 565, SHF 628)

For all the saints (HON 134)

Alleluia, sing to Jesus (HAMNS 262, HTC 170)

Collect and Post communion prayer

Advent 2000 to Advent 2001	The Proper 4 service material is not required for these years
Advent 2003 to Advent 2004	

Sunday between 5 and 11 June

(if after Trinity Sunday)

Proper 5

 ### Readings

Continuous

1 Kings 17.8-16[17-24]

The widow of Zarephath feeds Elijah before she feeds herself or her son with the last of the food she has. Had she heard God's command before the prophet came or did she believe the man of God's promise that the rains were to come and the drought end? We cannot be sure, but what is certain is that God's generosity is confirmed as promised.

or Related

1 Kings 17.17-24

The widow's son dies and she blames Elijah. His prayer of entreaty is answered and the child is restored to life. The miracle of her son's resurrection restores the widow's faith in the prophet.

Galatians 1.11-24

Paul insists that the gospel he received came directly from Christ himself. The testimony is to God, who can work through a person such as himself, who once persecuted the Church with the same fervour with which he is now preaching the gospel. Paul answers to no one except God.

Luke 7.11-17

Another widow and another dead son, this time at Nain. There is no prophet present here, but instead the carpenter Christ. Compassion is mentioned but not faith, and yet resurrection follows. The son is returned to his mother as happened at Zarephath. God is glorified here too and his presence recognized. Reports of what Christ has done spread like fire in the countryside.

 ### Talk/address/ sermon

Belief in resurrection requires faith and trust. These are first and foremost the qualities of the child. As Jesus himself taught, 'Unless you become as a little child . . .' It is not always easy to see the way ahead, especially in times of trouble such as unemployment, sickness or bereavement. But at the heart of the resurrection story is the knowledge that God is with us always.

What then does the resurrection mean for us as individuals and as a faith community? Which parts of our lives need resurrection? How might we tackle this?

 ### Congregational/ group activities

- Draw pictures or make masks of sad and happy faces. Use them in mime or acting out stories of sad-then-happy-ending stories. Identify sad and happy occasions in life. How can Christians bring about happy endings?

- Draw, or make models or collage pictures of resurrection symbols such as eggs, chicks, caterpillars or flies.

- Make butterfly shapes and decorate them. On the back, write or draw happy things to give thanks for. Construct them into a mobile to be used in the worship for the address/sermon or the intercessions.

Prayers/intercessions

Write out prayer headings on acetate OHPs, or use pictures or newspaper headlines concerning places or people for whom prayers may be offered. Alternatively, use the prayers prepared during the group activities.

Leader   The Lord is my strength and my song.

All   **He has become my salvation.**

Say the following creed, or affirmation of faith, together:

Do you believe and trust in God the Father,
who made all things?

We believe and trust in him.

Do you believe and trust in his Son Jesus Christ,
who redeemed the world?

We believe and trust in him.

Do you believe and trust in his Holy Spirit,
who gives life to the people of God?

We believe and trust in him.

This is the faith of the Church.

This is our faith.

We believe and trust in one God,

Father, Son and Holy Spirit. Amen.

Patterns for Worship, p. 58

Stories and other resources

Philip Welsh, 'Harold the reluctant mole', in *The Reluctant Mole and Other Beastly Tales*, Scripture Union, 1979

Leslie Francis and Nicola Slee, *Autumn: Betsy Bear Learns About Death,* NCEC, 1996

'The resurrection', in *Building New Bridges* (p. 78)

'Lazarus', in *Building New Bridges* (p. 100)

'Making it better', in *Under Fives – Alive!* (p. 38)

'Resurrection', in *Pick and Mix* (p. 147)

Music

Stay with me (HON 458, MT2 p. 67)

Be still and know that I am God (HON 52)

Bless the Lord, my soul (HON 61, MT2 p. 9)

Jesus' love is very wonderful (JU p. 14)

Christ's is the world in which we move (HON 83)

Immortal love, for ever full (HAMNS 133, HON 243, HTC 105)

Father of heav'n, whose love profound (HAMNS 97, HON 124, HTC 359)

Collect and post communion prayer

Advent 2000 to Advent 2001	The Proper 5 service material is not required for these years
Advent 2003 to Advent 2004	

Sunday between 12 and 18 June

(if after Trinity Sunday)

Proper 6

 ### Readings

Continuous

1 Kings 21.1-10[11-14]15-21a

Naboth refuses to sell King Ahab his vineyard. When Jezebel, King Ahab's wife, discovers what has happened to her husband, she masterminds Naboth's death. The prophet Elijah prophesies against Jezebel and Ahab for their wicked actions.

or Related

2 Samuel 11.26 – 12.10,13-15

This passage begins directly after the death of Bathsheba's husband. The prophet Nathan goes to King David and tells him the story of a rich man stealing a poor man's lamb for his feast, rather than taking one from his own plentiful flock. The comparison is made between the rich man's actions and those of David; judgement is promised on the king's household.

Galatians 2.15-21

Paul argues that we are justified by faith in Jesus Christ, rather than by observing the Law. He explains that we have been crucified with Christ and the life we now live is by faith in the Son of God, who loves us and gives himself for us.

Luke 7.36 – 8.3

Jesus is invited to have dinner at the home of Simon, a Pharisee. A woman, who has 'led a sinful life', wets Jesus' feet with her tears and then anoints them with perfume. Simon disapproves, but Jesus reproves him, stating that the woman's deep repentance has enabled her sins to be forgiven.

 ### Talk/address/ sermon

Ask one of the groups to act out the Gospel reading. What did it feel like to have your own feet anointed? What did it feel like to be forgiven? How would the woman have felt in the Gospel reading? How might our response to Jesus differ if we have been forgiven little or much?

 ### Congregational/ group activities

- Make large placards or banners for the five sections of intercessions (the Church/World/ Community/Sick/Those who have died).

- Smelling games. Bring in bottles of perfume, washing-up liquid, strong-smelling fluids. Cover up the labels on the bottles. Can they guess what is in the bottles?

- Enact the drama of the story from the Gospel reading in preparation for the talk.

- Use appropriate activities that were given for the Fifth Sunday in Lent.

Prayers/ intercessions

Use the large placards made earlier in the groups. Hold up the appropriate picture when praying for that particular topic.

Use the following confessions from the Iona community:

Together in worship, we face what we might not face alone

— that we are greedy, but fail to love our bodies

— that we are selfish, but fail to love ourselves

— that we are lazy, but fail to work for peace

— that we are human, but fail to love the earth

these we share in silence as we remember

our own faults and failings . . .

Silence

God of the turning tide

change us so that the energy of your forgiveness

flows into bold and joyful action

into a humility which is not defeatism

into the strength and confidence to be vulnerable.

David Coleman, in *The Pattern of Our Days*
(no. 26, p. 122)

Stories and other resources

Further suggestions for leading intercessions can be found in John Muir and Betty Pedley, *Children in the Church?*, NS/CHP, 1997

The Pattern of Our Days (no. 26, p. 122)

'Forgiveness', in *Pick and Mix* (p. 64)

Drama

Michael Forster, 'Corruption in high places', in *Act Two*, Kevin Mayhew, 1996

Michael Forster, 'Silly, snobbish Simon', in *Act Two*, Kevin Mayhew, 1996

Music

God forgave my sin in Jesus' name (HON 167, SHF 126)

I danced in the morning (HON 228)

Kyrie, Kyrie, eleison (HON 290, MT1 p. 55)

Come and see, come and see (HON 88)

Just as I am, without one plea (HAMNS 246, HON 287, HTC 440, SHF 304)

There's a wideness in God's mercy (HON 501)

Lord God, your love has called us here (HAMNS 489, HTC 480)

Collect and post communion prayer

Advent 2000 to Advent 2001	Use the collect and post communion prayer for the First Sunday after Trinity on page 130
Advent 2003 to Advent 2004	

Sunday between 19 and 25 June

(if after Trinity Sunday)

Proper 7

 ### Readings

Continuous

1 Kings 19.1-4[5-7]8-15a

Jezebel threatens to kill Elijah. He flees, taking his servant with him. Once out in the safety of the desert Elijah tells God that he has had enough. But the Lord provides him with food and drink and prepares him for the next task that he wants him to do.

or Related

Isaiah 65.1-9

God makes himself known to all kinds of people – even those who are not looking for him. But they ignore and reject him and continue to lead sinful lives. God threatens to punish these wayward people but promises to allow some of the children of Israel to escape this punishment.

Luke 8.26-39

Jesus meets a pitiful man possessed by a demon. He is naked, lives in the tombs, is violent and dangerous and controlled by a league of demons. Jesus calls for the demons to leave the man. They beg Jesus not to send them to the abyss. They ask to be sent into some pigs instead. Jesus grants their request. The community should have thanked Jesus for freeing their neighbourhood from this dangerous man, but instead they beg Jesus to leave.

Galatians 3.23-29

Before Christ came people could only live by the Law, given to Moses by God. But Jesus is the way through which we can be put right with God through faith. God has no favourites and his blessings and freedom are available to all.

 ### Talk/address/ sermon

Jesus the healer cares for his people and wants them to be whole and free from all that torments them. Develop the theme of Jesus not simply wanting to cure a disease but to make the sufferer whole. It is sin that keeps us from wholeness.

The man known as 'Legion' is healed, yet Jesus does not allow him to stay with him. Instead, he is told to return home and to report all that God has done for him to the people who know him. Who are the people God has sent us to share the good news with? Which of our friends/neighbours/people at work or school can we especially pray for?

 ### Congregational/ group activities

- Make a collage or banner using pictures or symbols of the different healing stories.

- Cut out large letters to spell WHOLE. Get children to write or draw things from the story depicting the desire of Jesus for us to be made whole.

- Play games which involve parts of a puzzle being put together to make a whole, e.g. cut birthday and Christmas cards in half. Mix them up and then ask the groups to match them to the correct pieces.

Prayers/ intercessions

Pray for:

- the sick in body, mind and spirit;

- those tormented by addiction;

- those bound by guilt of sin.

Leader   Loving Father God:

All   **set your children free.**

Use the following responses to pray for those in need of God's healing:

Saviour God, we pray for those who are sick. We lift them up to you, Lord.

Hold them and heal them, we pray.

We pray for those who are mourning the death of people they love. We lift them up to you, Lord.

Hold them and heal them, we pray.

We pray for those who are homeless, hungry or helplessly poor. We lift them up to you, Lord.

Hold them and heal them, we pray.

We pray for those who are lonely or unloved. We lift them up to you, Lord.

Hold them and heal them, we pray.

We pray for those who suffer because they spread the good news about Jesus. We lift them up to you, Lord.

Hold them and heal them, we pray.

We pray for those who don't know where to turn for help. We lift them up to you, Lord.

Hold them and heal them, we pray.

A Church for All Ages (p. 168)

Use the prayers in *Prayers for the People*, The Caring/Church/Healing section on pages 82–7.

Stories and other resources

'Healing', in *The Pattern of Our Days* (p. 46)

'Healing', in *Pick and Mix* (p. 77)

'A man through the roof!', in *Building New Bridges* (p. 91)

Peter Graystone and Eileen Turner, *A Church for All Ages* (p. 168)

Leslie Francis and Nicola Slee, *The Grumpy Day*, NCEC, 1994

Prayer books on healing, such as *Prayers for Help and Healing* by William Barclay, Font, 1968

Nicola Currie and Jean Thomson, 'Elijah hears a still small voice', *In the Beginning*, NS/CHP, 1995

Michael Perry and Pat Goodland, *Prayers for the People,* Marshall Pickering, 1992

Stories about freedom and release ('Cadbury', in *Together with Children*, February 1996)

 ## Music

Abba, Father, let me be (HON 5, SHF 1)

Be still and know (SHF 37)

Love beyond measure (SHF 352)

May your loving Spirit (BBP 45)

The love of God (BBP 58)

For the healing of the nations (HAMNS 361, HON 139)

O worship the Lord in the beauty of holiness (HAMNS 49, HON 394)

The prophets spoke in days of old (HAMNS 513)

Collect and post communion prayer

Advent 2000 to Advent 2001	Use the collect and post communion prayer for the Second Sunday after Trinity on page 130
Advent 2003 to Advent 2004	

Sunday between 26 June and 2 July

Proper 8

 ### Readings

Continuous

2 Kings 2.1,2,6-14

Elijah prepares for the end of his earthly life. His successor, Elisha, asks for a 'double portion' of his spirit. Elijah is taken up to heaven in a chariot of fire.

or Related

1 Kings 19.15,16,19-21

Elijah receives the message from the Lord to anoint several kings and to anoint Elisha as his successor. Elijah goes and finds Elisha, who prepares to follow him.

Luke 9.51-62

The disciples show a lack of love for believers outside their own group but Jesus rebukes them. Three men could have become disciples but they would not meet the conditions that Jesus laid down.

Galatians 5.1,13-25

Christ has freed us from the slavery of the Law. This freedom which Christ offers is not about selfish indiscipline, it is about living life as dictated by the law of love and God's Holy Spirit. Paul lists the fruits of the Spirit.

 ### Talk/address/sermon

Use the sheets on the characteristics of the disciples that were prepared earlier by the groups. Discuss how each of the disciples brought different abilities and personalities to Jesus' group.

'Disciple' refers to one who accepts the words of the teacher and becomes his follower. What are the marks of a Christian disciple? What are the spiritual essentials for discipleship?

 ### Congregational/group activities

- Make footprints. On each one write a word associated with the cost/privilege of discipleship. Lay the trail of footprints and invite people to walk over the trail thinking about or speaking out loud the words written on the footprints.

- Make badges in a footprint shape. Inscribe the words on them, 'I'm following Jesus'.

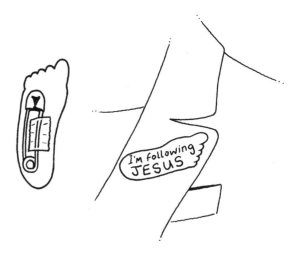

- Organize a procession or journey to follow a trail of footsteps, 'Walking in the Steps of Jesus'. Have different parts of the church as challenge points. As the journeying people arrive ask them if they want to go on with Jesus or turn back.

- Give each group the name of one of the disciples of Christ and a sheet of paper. Ask them to write up some words that describe this person but not to put his name on the paper. (Provide biblical passages on these disciples if necessary.) Use these at the beginning of the talk, to see if others in the congregation can identify the disciple from these descriptions.

Prayers/intercessions

Use the following responses:

Pharisees and wicked men,
Jesus loves them all,
Saints and sinners, now and then,
Jesus loves them all,
Every country, everywhere,
Jesus loves them all,
People no one else can bear,
Jesus loves them all,
Every type of hair or skin,
Jesus loves them all,
Short or giant, thick or thin,
Jesus loves them all,
Good at school or with a ball,
Jesus loves them all,
Good at nothing much at all,
Jesus loves them all,
Poor or rich, between the two,
Jesus loves them all,
Help us love them just like you,
Jesus loves them all. Amen.

A Church for All Ages (p. 162)

Use the prayers in *Prayers for the People*, 'Following Jesus' section on pages 20–4.

Stories and other resources

More general stories about discipleship and the Christian life: Sue Relf, *100 Instant Children's Talks*, (Kingsway, 1994), Section 7: Stories 70–92

A Church for All Ages (p. 162)

Michael Perry and Pat Goodland, *Prayers for the People*, Marshall Pickering, 1992

Story of Pilgrim, in *All Aboard!* (Section 7:04–16)

'Hands and feet', in *Under Fives – Alive!* (p. 29)

'Disciples', in *Pick and Mix* (pp. 52–3)

'Pilgrimage and journeys', in *The Pattern of Our Days*

Music

God's Spirit is in my heart (HON 180)

Wherever you go I will follow (BBP 16)

Will you come and follow me (HON 560)

We really want to thank you Lord (SHF 587)

Always remember, never forget (BBP 1)

O Jesus, I have promised (HAMNS 235, HON 372, HTC 531, SHF 400)

Take my life, and let it be (HAMNS 249, HON 464, HTC 554, SHF 496)

Be thou my guardian and my guide (HAMNS 217, HON 55)

Collect and post communion prayer

Advent 2000 to Advent 2001	Use the collect and post communion prayer for the Third Sunday after Trinity on page 131
Advent 2003 to Advent 2004	

Sunday between 3 and 9 July

Proper 9

 ## Readings

Continuous

2 Kings 5.1-14

Naaman, a Syrian leader and soldier, was suffering from a severe skin disease. His Israelite servant–girl suggests he should see the prophet Elisha. Elisha tells Naaman to wash in the River Jordan seven times. At first Naaman refuses to do this but when he does, he is healed.

Isaiah 66.10-14

The writer urges us to rejoice with Jerusalem and be glad for her. The Lord will extend peace and wealth to her and Jerusalem will comfort her people, like a mother comforts her child.

Galatians 6.[1-6]7-16

Paul reminds us that we get what we deserve. We should do good and live our lives according to God's Spirit – not our natural desires. Paul emphasizes the importance of being made new to Christ and not external things.

Luke 10.1-11,16-20

Jesus chooses 72 disciples and sends them out in pairs to visit the surrounding towns and villages. He instructs them to take greetings of 'peace' to the households they visit.

 ## Talk/address/ sermon

The mission of the Church. We are called to be the bearers of the good news. How do we live out our faith in our life, work and family? Mission is the work not just of a small group but of all Christians. What is God calling us to do and say? To whom? How can we identify what we are called to do: as individuals and as a church?

 ## Congregational/ group activities

- Draw a simple map to illustrate the Gospel reading. Mark on the houses. Put different coloured stickers representing the disciples. Put two stickers to each house. Estimate how many people would be reached by their visit.

- Identify examples of good news. How many ways can you find to tell others? What could you tell others about Jesus? Make posters, adverts and newspaper headlines to publicize your message.

- Give each person a paper plate. Ask them to draw pictures of people (or events) to pray for on these plates. Adults might also write a full prayer for the person or event on the back of the plates.

Prayers/ intercessions

To pray for the world: Lay out on the floor the largest map of the world that you can find. Play some Taizé music in the background while the congregation write their own short prayers for a specific country (or person from another country). They then come and place the prayers on the map.

To pray for people at home: During a time of quiet, or as music plays in the background, invite members of the congregation to bring the paper plates with the drawings and prayers on them and place them on the altar or display board at the front.

Stories and other resources

Philip Welsh, 'Harold the reluctant mole', *The Reluctant Mole and Other Beastly Tales*, Scripture Union, 1979

Nicola Currie and Jean Thomson, 'Naaman is cured', *In the Beginning*, NS/CHP, 1995

'Journeys', in *Pick and Mix* (pp. 96–7)

'Disciples', in *Pick and Mix* (pp. 52–3)

'How Mark brought the good news', *Festive Allsorts* (p. 27)

'Philip and James', *Festive Allsorts* (p. 28)

All Aboard! for pilgrimage activities

 ## Music

Dona Nobis Pacem (MT2 p. 28)

One more step along the world I go (HON 405)

Be bold, be strong (JU p. 40)

Make me a channel of your peace (HON 328)

Go, tell it on the mountain (HON 165)

How sweet the name of Jesus sounds (HAMNS 122, HON 220, HTC 211)

O for a thousand tongues to sing (HAMNS 125, HON 362, HTC 219)

Go forth and tell! (HON 164, HTC 505)

Collect and post communion prayer

Advent 2000 to Advent 2001	Use the collect and post communion prayer for the Fourth Sunday after Trinity on page 131
Advent 2003 to Advent 2004	

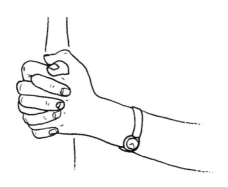

Sunday between 10 and 16 July

Proper 10

Readings

Continuous

Amos 7.7-17

The prophet sees the Lord standing by a wall, with a plumb–line in his hand. He is told that the plumb-line has been set against the people of Israel and they have been found wanting.

or Related

Deuteronomy 30.9-14

When Moses gives the people the Law, God makes it clear that keeping it is not an impossible task. God helps us to obey this Law and we are urged to know God's Law in order to obey it.

Colossians 1.1-14

Paul greets the Colossians and affirms their faith. He encourages them to be strong and to do what pleases God.

Luke 10.25-37

The parable of the Good Samaritan. Who is our neighbour? It is through our actions that real love is shown. In this parable a number of people who might have been expected to care for someone in need pass by and it is the person least expected who stops and shows practical love.

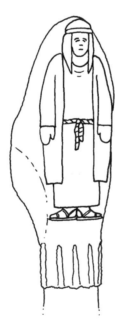

Talk/address/sermon

Begin with a dramatic presentation that has been prepared in the group activities.

The question of 'Who is my neighbour?' is still very relevant. We tend to be selective about who our 'neighbours' are. Churches happily send harvest gifts to old people's homes, but what about probation/down-and-out hostels? And why only send gifts at harvest?

What about other faiths and denominations in our town, or the homeless/mentally ill? How much do we know about them and how much do they know about us? How might we reach out to enrich, and be enriched by others?

Congregational/group activities

- Prepare a simple dramatic presentation of the story either mimed to the words being read slowly, or to music. If you are feeling creative, make some puppets. Paper plates on sticks or sock-covered hands are the simplest.

- Discuss in groups who is our neighbour and what makes a good neighbour. Why do you think the scribe and the Pharisee passed by in the story? Who are our neighbours?

- Role-play situations where, like the Good Samaritan, we might be asked to help those in need (in situations such as homelessness, drugs, fair trade). What can be done as a church, or in our households?

 ## Prayers/ intercessions

Identify the congregational concerns – local, national and international.

Use the response:

Leader   Father, our world is troubled.

All   **Send down your Spirit of love.**

Use the following prayer. It links closely with the Gospel reading and with the theme of Christ, the friend of sinners, gathering together people of every nation to worship him:

Living God, Father of light,
Hope of nations, Friend of sinners,
Builder of the city that is to come;
your love is made visible in Jesus Christ,
you bring home the lost, restore the sinner
and give dignity to the despised.
In the face of Jesus Christ
your light shines out,
flooding lives with goodness and truth,
gathering into one a divided and broken humanity.
With people from every race and nation,
with the Church of all the ages,
with apostles, evangelists and martyrs
we join the angels of heaven
in their unending song:
Holy, holy, holy Lord,
God of power and might,
heaven and earth are full of your glory.
Hosanna in the highest.
Blessed is he who comes in the name of the Lord.
Hosanna in the highest.

Patterns for Worship (p. 145)

Use the prayers in the 'Brokenness and wholeness' section in *The Pattern of Our Days*.

 ## Stories and other resources

Anita Haigh, 'Modern parable of the Good Samaritan: a poem', in *Rap, Rhyme and Reason*, Scripture Union, 1996

'Brokenness and wholeness' (p. 50), in *The Pattern of Our Days*

'The good Samaritan', in *Praise, Play and Paint* (p. 93)

'Neighbours', in *Pick and Mix* (p. 119)

 ## Drama

Dave Hopwood, 'Samaritan rap', in *Acting Up*, NS/CHP, 1995

 ## Music

Ubi Caritas (MT1 p. 28)

Jesus' hands were kind hands (JP 134)

When I needed a neighbour (HON 548)

My Lord, what love is this (HON 345)

Caring, sharing (BBP 8)

Loving Jesus, we will thank you (BBP 6)

Hark, my soul, it is the Lord (HAMNS 244, HON 197, HTC 472)

Christ is the world's true light (HAMNS 440, HON 78, HTC 321)

Father, Lord of all creation (HAMNS 356, HON 122)

Collect and post communion prayer

Advent 2000 to Advent 2001	Use the collect and post communion prayer for the Fifth Sunday after Trinity on page 131
Advent 2003 to Advent 2004	

Sunday between 17 and 23 July

Proper 11

 ### Readings

Continuous

Amos 8.1-12

The prophet is shown another image by the Lord: a basket of ripe fruit. He is told that, like the fruit, the people of Israel are ripe for plucking and will be spared no more.

or Related

Genesis 18.1-10a

Abraham and Sarah welcome three strangers who visit them. They go to the trouble to provide a meal and make the visitors welcome. The visitors bring a blessing to Abraham and Sarah telling them that they will have a son.

Colossians 1.15-28

Christ is portrayed as supreme over all. By him all things were created and in him all things are held together. Through him we have also been reconciled with God.

Luke 10.38-42

Jesus visits Martha and Mary. Mary sits to listen to Jesus but Martha busies herself in the kitchen and feels overburdened. Jesus reminds Martha that it is important to spend time with him.

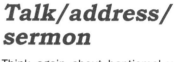 ### Talk/address/ sermon

Think again about baptismal vows. Do we live them out in our everyday lives? What, in reality, does 'grow in faith' mean to us? Explore further the horticultural metaphor of growing and being rooted. What about 'nurturing', 'pruning', 'weeding' and 'feeding'?

 ### Congregational/ group activities

- Ask the group to list their favourite foods or meals. Give them paper plates, tissue paper and any scrap material. Ask them to design a 'meal' on their paper plates using these materials.

- Play listening games. Tape a number of sounds (such as a siren, alarm, bells, baby crying) and ask the groups to identify the sounds.

- Make 'promise boxes' or wallets with words of Jesus to look at each day.
- Make a 'thank-you' book. Give each group some blank sheets of paper or card stapled together. Ask each member of the group to draw a picture of something they can thank God for and stick these into the book.

Prayers/ intercessions

Use the 'thank-you' book made earlier as a basis for a time of thanksgiving.

Alternatively, use 'thank-you' prayers from a collection of prayers for children. Two examples are given below:

And God created us in his own image

God, you have given us many of your gifts:
the gift of beauty;
the gift of wonder;
the gift of creation;
the gift of life itself.
Thank you for sharing so much of yourself with us;
may we share ourselves with you.

Pattern of God's presence

When I wake up in the morning,
thank you, God, for being there.
When I come to school each day,
thank you, God, for being there.
When I am playing with my friends,
thank you, God, for being there.
And when I go to bed at night,
thank you, God, for being there.

Prayers for Children
(no. 45, p. 41 and no. 47, p. 44)

Stories and other resources

Leslie Francis and Nicola Slee, *Water: Teddy Horsley and Baptism*, NCEC, 1996

'Mary and Martha', in *Building New Bridges* (p. 96)

John Greenhalgh, *Thank You God*, Scripture Union, 1987

Diana Murrie and Steve Pearce, 'Celebration' (sheet 9), 'Food of belonging' (sheet 14), in *Children and Holy Communion*

Christopher Herbert, 'People', in *Prayers for Children*, NS/CHP, 1993 (p. 42)

'Choices' (p. 31), and 'Meals' (p. 116), in *Pick and Mix*

Music

Jesus, Jesus here I am (JU p. 96)

When I feel the touch (HON 546)

Oh! Oh! Oh! how good is the Lord (HON 397)

Good morning, Jesus (BBP 28)

Emmanuel (SHF 79)

Jesus, name above all names (SHF 288)

Man of Sorrows! what a name (SHF 361)

Take my life, and let it be (HAMNS 249, HON 464, HTC 554, SHF 496)

O King enthroned on high (HAMNS 158, HON 373)

Collect and post communion prayer

Advent 2000 to Advent 2001	Use the collect and post communion prayer for the Sixth Sunday after Trinity on page 132
Advent 2003 to Advent 2004	

Sunday between 24 and 30 July

Proper 12

 ### Readings

Continuous

Hosea 1.2-10

The prophet receives the command to marry an adulterous wife. Each of Hosea's children are then given a name symbolizing the unfaithfulness of the Israelite people in following their God. Yet the passage ends with the promise that the Israelites will become as numerous as the sands of the sea and again be called 'sons of the living God'.

or Related

Genesis 18.20-32

Abraham is told by the Lord that his descendants will become a great and powerful nation. In stark contrast, the destruction of Sodom and Gomorrah is foretold. Abraham pleads for the people of Sodom and is promised that, even if only ten righteous people are found there, the city will be spared.

Colossians 2.6-15[16-19]

Paul prays for the people of Colossae and urges them to continue to grow in the knowledge of God, so that they may have great endurance and patience.

Luke 11.1-13

Jesus teaches his disciples how to pray, using words that have become familiarly known as the Lord's Prayer. He then stresses the importance of persistent prayer.

 ### Talk/address/ sermon

Choose several adults and children to come to the front of the church. Explain that you are considering making large name badges for all members of the church, so they can learn each other's names. Give a large sheet with the wrong name on to each volunteer and introduce them with this name. Then apologize for mixing them up. Ask them how it felt to be called by the wrong name.

Why are names so important to us? Does anyone know the real meaning of their name? Explain the names Hosea's children were given and why. Talk about the change Jesus has brought in our relationship with God – that we can now call him by the name of Father.

 ### Congregational/ group activities

- Have cut-out pieces of card with names of people and their real 'meanings' mixed up. The groups try to sort out which meanings go with which names, e.g. Jonathan with 'God has given'. You might want to use the names of people in the congregation, or just biblical names for this activity.

- Make 'personalized' biscuits or cakes by decorating them with glacé icing (mixing together icing sugar with a small amount of hot water, until the icing is smooth enough to be spread with a knife). People might like to put their initials or first names on the biscuits, using Smarties or other small sweets.

- Produce a simple poster with a version of the Lord's Prayer on it.

- Write prayers based on each part of the Lord's Prayer (praying for our own needs under headings such as 'Give us this day our daily bread', or for forgiveness under the title 'Forgive us our sins').

- Learn the sign-language actions that accompany the song 'Our Father who is in heaven'.

- Begin a display called 'The Journey of Faith', which will be added to over the next few weeks. Make the background to the display from green and black cloths (for grass and night sky) and add drawings of the hills and Abraham.

Prayers/ intercessions

Use the fingers on a hand to explain the different types of prayer:

- **praise** – thumb that points upwards to heaven;

- **confession** – first finger that points to yourself;

- **thanksgiving** – the second and longest finger, to remember the many things we can thank God for;

- **prayer for others** – the third, ring finger, where we often wear rings to remember our relationship to others;

- **prayer for ourselves** – the fourth and smallest finger.

Pray a short prayer, using the fingers to illustrate each type of prayer.

Read slowly through the Lord's Prayer, pausing after each line. Use the prayers written earlier in the groups at the appropriate point.

Stories and other resources

Books on prayer relating to everyday life, such as Martin Wallace, *Pocket Celtic Prayers*, NS/CHP, 1996

Versions of the Lord's Prayer for children, such as the one in the *Little Bible Window Prayers* series, Nelson Word Ltd, 1994

'Prayer', in *Pick and Mix* (p. 135)

'Names' (sheet 7) 'Prayers' (sheet 12) and 'When you pray' (sheet 13) in *Children and Holy Communion*

Leslie Francis and Diane Drayson, Section 26, 'Picnic time', from *Bread for All God's Family*, Gracewing, 1997

Drama

Dave Hopwood, 'Prayer is like breathing', in *Acting Up*, NS/CHP, 1995

Anita Haigh, 'Arfer (The Lord's Prayer)' in *Rap, Rhyme and Reason*, Scripture Union, 1996

Dave Hopwood, 'Persistent widow', in *A Fistful of Sketches*, NS/CHP, 1996

 ## Music

Ask and it shall be given (SHF 20)

Father, I give you the whole of my life (SHF 93)

In my life, Lord, be glorified (SHF 216)

Our Father who is in heaven (JU p. 94)

Prayer is like a telephone (JU p. 28)

Come, Lord Jesus, come (JU p. 88)

Our Father, who art in heaven (traditional Caribbean – HON 411)

Thy kingdom come, O God (HAMNS 177, HON 519)

Lord, teach us how to pray aright (HAMNS 227, HTC 367)

Collect and post communion prayer

Advent 2000 to Advent 2001	Use the collect and post communion prayer for the Seventh Sunday after Trinity on page 132
Advent 2003 to Advent 2004	

Sunday between 24 and 30 July

Sunday between 31 July and 6 August

Proper 13

 Readings

Continuous

Hosea 11.1-11

God's love for Israel is proclaimed and compared with that of a parent to a child. Although it was God who taught Ephraim to walk and led them with 'cords of human kindness, with ties of love', they were still determined to turn away. God's compassion is aroused towards them and the passage ends with the powerful image of the Israelites' return to him.

or Related

Ecclesiastes 1.2,12-14; 2.18-23

The Teacher views all life as utterly meaningless. He discusses the merits of wisdom and folly and then turns his attention to the everyday life of work. Even this is seen to be meaningless, as there can be no way of knowing whether one's work will be passed on and continued by a wise man or a fool.

Colossians 3.1-11

Paul reminds the people of Colossae that since Christ has been raised from death, their hearts and minds should be set on things above and not on earthly things. They should rid themselves of everything that belongs to the earthly nature. Their new nature should transform the way they relate together, banishing lying and deceit. For Christ has broken down the barriers between Greek and Jew, slave and free.

Luke 12.13-21

The parable of the rich fool. One of the crowd following Jesus wants his brother to divide an inheritance and tries to use Jesus as a judge in the situation. Jesus responds by telling the parable of the rich fool. In the parable, the fool decides to tear down his barns and build bigger ones, to store up his riches for a life of ease and merriment. God calls him a fool for thinking only of himself, for that same night his life will be demanded from him.

 Talk/address/ sermon

Hold up adverts cut from recent news-papers/magazines, trying to persuade us to buy bigger, better, faster, more impressive products.

Talk about the pressures placed on us never to be content with what we have, but always to seek more. What can we learn about true wisdom and folly from these passages? What do they teach us about the way of life Jesus intends us to lead? What priorities should it give us in life?

 Congregational/ group activities

* Discuss in small groups: What is foolish behaviour? Who is considered a fool in our society and are they really the true fools? List five foolish and five wise aspects of our society.

* Draw up a list of all the things we consider basic necessities for our own lifestyle. Compare this list with the basic essentials of someone living in a much poorer country.

* Add to the display on 'The Journey of Faith', focusing on the life of one saint from the past (this might be the patron saint of your church). Draw pictures and write out some of the details of his or her life story. Add these to one side of the display.

* Make a collage, on one side sticking pictures of the basic essentials for life and on the other the luxuries that we enjoy.

Prayers/ intercessions

Focus on praying for those who work on development or aid projects, and for those living in poverty.

Use the response:

Leader   In your mercy

All   **forgive us our greed.**

Use the Confession from *The Pattern of Our Days* (no. 26, p. 122).

Stories and other resources

'Understanding', in *Pick and Mix* (p. 164) (the story 'The Prince and the Blind Men' from this chapter is particularly appropriate)

Drama

Derek Haylock, 'The rich fool', in *Plays for All Seasons*, NS/CHP, 1997

Paul Burbridge and Murray Watts, in 'The wisdom and folly rap', *Divine Comedies*, Monarch, 1994

Anita Haigh, 'Ballad of the rich fool', in *Rap, Rhyme and Reason*, Scripture Union, 1996

 Music

O Lord, you are my light (SHF 412)

He has arisen, alleluia (WP 51)

Sing Hallelujah to the Lord (SHF 476)

God's not dead, (No!) he is alive (JU p. 38)

Be thou my vision (HAMNS 343, HON 56, HTC 545, SHF 38)

Praise to the holiest in the height (HAMNS 117, HON 426, HTC 140, SHF 450)

Thou whose almighty word (HAMNS 180, HON 514, HTC 506)

Collect and post communion prayer

Advent 2000 to Advent 2001	Use the collect and post communion prayer for the Eighth Sunday after Trinity on page 132
Advent 2003 to Advent 2004	

Sunday between 7 and 13 August

Proper 14

 ### Readings

Continuous

Isaiah 1.1,10-20

This vision of Isaiah's begins with a denouncement of the rulers of Sodom and the people of Judah. The multitude of sacrifices that they offer to the Lord are seen as meaningless. The Lord refuses to listen to their prayers until they stop doing wrong and start doing right. They are urged to seek justice and support those who cannot care for themselves. Even though their sins are great they can still be forgiven, on the condition that they are willing and obedient.

or Related

Genesis 15.1-6

God makes his covenant with Abram. Even though Abram is childless, he is told that his descendants will be as numerous as the stars. Abram's faith in God is 'credited to him as righteousness'.

Hebrews 11.1-3,8-16

Faith is explained as being sure of what we hope for and certain of what we do not see. The writer then uses the story of Abraham to illustrate this faith in action.

Luke 12.32-40

Jesus tells his disciples to sell their possessions and give to the poor, so that they can concentrate on the treasures of heaven. They are told to be watchful and ready for the coming of the Son of man, like servants waiting for their master to return from a wedding banquet.

 ### Talk/address/ sermon

Interview a member of the congregation about their faith. How can they believe in someone they cannot see? What difference does their faith make to the way they live?

 ### Congregational/ group activities

- 'Trust' games. As a follow-up to the Hebrews reading, use one of the many 'trust' games to illustrate faith in action. For example, blindfold a volunteer and direct them with vocal instructions around the church. Ensure there are no painful obstacles in the way!

- Discussion. What are the main concerns in our own area: homelessness, debt, family breakdown, public transport? In what ways can we 'seek justice' and support those in need as a church?

- Send off to Tear Fund, Christian Aid or other suitable charities for material on justice and poverty. Show their slides or video to the group, or use it instead of the talk.

- Continue work on 'The Journey of Faith' display. Have each person draw a star shape (or have templates ready for this). Each person should put their name in the centre of the star and decorate it. Place these stars against the sky background.

Prayers/ intercessions

Focus on the areas of need in your own local community, especially those that were discussed in the small groups.

Use the response:

Leader   Father, for these things

All   **we trust in you.**

Use the following responses to pray for God's grace to act in the hearts, lives and wills of the congregation:

O God, we are your people: in your Son you have redeemed us; by your Spirit you have sealed us as your own.

Make our hearts respond to your love.
Lord, receive our praise,
and hear our prayer.

Make our lives bear witness to your mercy.
Lord, receive our praise,
and hear our prayer.

Make our wills ready to obey.
Lord, receive our praise,
and hear our prayer.

Show us your glory,
that we may delight in your presence,
and walk with you faithfully
all our days. Amen.

Michael Perry, in *Church Family Worship* (no. 126)

Stories and other resources

Nicola Currie and Jean Thomson, 'The call of Abraham', in *In the Beginning*, NS/CHP, 1995

The 'Invitation to Faith' section in *Church Family Worship* (nos. 388–412)

Drama

Dave Hopwood, 'The Canaan chorus', in *Acting Up*, NS/CHP, 1995

Stuart Thomas, 'Abraham – Mr Faith', *Keep It in the Family*, Kevin Mayhew, 1993

Music

God be in my head, and in my understanding (HAMNS 236, HON 166, HTC 543)

Have faith in God, my heart (HAMNS 372, HON 201, HTC 431)

I believe in God the Father (HTC 434)

Father, I place into your hands (SHF 94)

Seek ye first the kingdom of God (SHF 471)

Father Abraham (JU p. 8)

He made the stars to shine (JU p. 70)

We are marching in the light of God (JU p. 34)

Collect and post communion prayer

Advent 2000 to Advent 2001	Use the collect and post communion prayer for the Ninth Sunday after Trinity on page 133
Advent 2003 to Advent 2004	

Sunday between 14 and 20 August

Proper 15

 ### Readings

Continuous

Isaiah 5.1-7

The Song of the Vineyard. The vineyard, that was carefully tended, is seen to yield only bad fruit. The people of Judah and Jerusalem are asked what more could have been done for the vineyard for it to bear good fruit. Now it will be destroyed and be made into a wasteland. In the same way, Israel and Judah have failed to bring forth the good fruit of justice and righteousness.

or Related

Jeremiah 23.23-29

The lies of false prophets are condemned. They are accused of prophesying from the delusions of their own minds. Their words pale in comparison to those of the Lord: powerful words like fire or a hammer that breaks a rock in pieces.

Hebrews 11.29 – 12.2

The writer continues to tell inspiring stories of faith from the past, including those of the Israelites passing through the Red Sea to escape the Egyptians, the destruction of Jericho and the many unnamed believers who have been persecuted for their faith. Being surrounded by such a cloud of witnesses, we are encouraged to concentrate wholly on Jesus and the tasks he has set for us.

Luke 12.49-56

Jesus talks of the difficult times ahead for those who follow him. He tells how families will be divided by their response to him. The crowd are called hypocrites for interpreting weather conditions, yet not knowing how to interpret what is taking place before their very eyes.

 ### Talk/address/ sermon

Choose people of different ages from the congregation – preferably a baby/toddler, primary-aged child, teenager, young parent and pensioner. Have appropriate items associated with each age group ready, e.g. nappy for baby, pension book or bus pass for pensioner.

Talk about the journey of life and what we encounter at each stage of our lives (use visual aids for each age range). Where is God in our journey? Is he closest to us when we are young and 'innocent' like a baby, or older and supposedly wiser as a pensioner? Is he furthest away when we're a teenager, or a parent? Place people in a close circle. Talk about how God remains at the centre throughout, however far away we feel he may be.

 ### Congregational/ group activities

- Draw or make a list of what you would take with you on a long journey. What has God given us to help us on our own journey of faith?

- The Hebrews reading lists a number of the heroes of faith in the Old Testament. Draw and write a short summary of their lives and add this to the display 'The Journey of Faith'.

- 'The Race of Life'. Use children's race games here (such as egg-and-spoon or sack races). Susan Sayers' *Focus the Word* mentions several of these (p. 263).

- Look at the life of one of the great Christian athletes, Eric Liddell. Show excerpts from the film *Chariots of Fire*.

Prayers/ intercessions

- Ask a family, housegroup or children's group to write a number of short prayers, including ones for those persecuted or suffering for their faith. Sing one of the Taizé 'Kyrie Eleisons' between each prayer.

- *Patterns for Worship* provides a number of examples of 'Kyrie Confessions' (a short sentence inserted between the petitions of the Kyrie). Use one of these during a time of confession or write your own sentence. An example is printed below:

God be gracious to us and bless us,
and make your face shine upon us:
Lord, have mercy.
Lord, have mercy.

May your ways be known on the earth,
your saving power among the nations:
Christ, have mercy.
Christ, have mercy.

You, Lord, have made known your salvation,
and reveal your justice in the sight of the nations:
Lord, have mercy.
Lord, have mercy.

Patterns for Worship (p. 48)

Stories and other resources

Susan Sayers, *Focus the Word* (p. 263), Kevin Mayhew, 1989

'Journeys', in *Pick and Mix* (p. 96)

Drama

Derek Haylock, 'Christian Olympics', in *Plays on the Word*, NS/CHP, 1993

Dave Hopwood, 'Careless talk', in *A Fistful of Sketches*, NS/CHP, 1996

 ## Music

My God is so big (JU p. 6)

Be bold, be strong (JU p. 40)

Kyrie, Kyrie, Eleison (HON 290, MT1 p. 55)

Therefore, since we have so great a cloud of witnesses (SHF 530)

Lord hear our prayer (BBP 4)

Be thou my guardian and my guide (HAMNS 217, HON 55)

Fight the good fight with all thy might (HAMNS 220, HON 128, HTC 526, SHF 103)

Stand up, stand up for Jesus (HAMNS 221, HON 457, HTC 535, SHF 489)

Collect and post communion prayer

Advent 2000 to Advent 2001	Use the collect and post communion prayer for the Tenth Sunday after Trinity on page 133
Advent 2003 to Advent 2004	

Sunday between 21 and 27 August

Proper 16

 ## Readings

Continuous

Jeremiah 1.4-10

Jeremiah is commissioned by the Lord to be his spokesman. Jeremiah is worried that he will not be fit for the task, and will not know how to speak. The Lord reassures him that he will always be with him and puts the very words into Jeremiah's mouth.

or Related

Isaiah 58.9b-14

The Israelites are given the conditional promise that, if they do away with the yoke of oppression and bring justice to the needy, the Lord will restore them and guide them always. Their people will rebuild the ancient ruins and feast on the inheritance that was once promised to Jacob.

Hebrews 12.18-29

The writer describes the awesome, terrifying occasion when the Law was first given to Moses. In contrast, the new covenant is based on the heavenly Jerusalem – a city of joy, rather than a mountain of burning fire.

Luke 13.10-17

On a Sabbath, Jesus heals a woman crippled for eighteen years. The synagogue ruler is indignant and tells the assembled people not to come on a Sabbath to be healed. Jesus responds by calling them hypocrites – they are willing on a Sabbath to untie their donkey so it might have water, but not for the needy to be healed.

 ## Talk/address/ sermon

Take in as many visual aids as you can find that are linked with health care (stethoscope, bandages, plasters, first aid kit, etc.). When do we need to use these items? Look at occasions when Jesus healed people. His miracles of healing were an outpouring of compassion on those in need, not just a physical healing of their illness. How can we help those who are ill? Why is it important that we should also pray for them?

Congregational/ group activities

- Discuss in small groups: What is it like to be ill? How would the woman have felt when Jesus healed her? Why did the synagogue ruler try to prevent any more healings on the Sabbath? How does the church pray for those who are ill?

- Draw pictures of those who care in the community. Interview a local doctor/nurse/health-care visitor about their work.

- Complete the display 'The Journey of Faith' with pictures or drawings of modern-day saints.

- Make 'get well' cards to send or deliver to people who are sick or are prayed for by name at your church.

Prayers/ intercessions

This would be an ideal opportunity to focus on praying for healing for individuals in the congregation.

Conclude with this prayer:

Almighty God,
we thank you for your mercy and your grace:
you are our light in darkness,
our strength in weakness,
and our comfort in sorrow.
You heal our bodies and our minds;
you ease our pain,
you lift our anxieties
and give us hope.
So fill us with your Spirit's power
that we may take your healing love
to a world in need,
and bring glory to your name;
through Jesus Christ our Lord. **Amen.**

Michael Perry, in *Church Family Worship* (no. 457)

Alternatively, use the intercessions from 'Brokenness and wholeness: a service of prayers for healing' (*The Pattern of Our Days* no. 9, p. 50).

Stories and other resources

'Healing', in *Pick and Mix* (p. 77)

'Healing', in *The Pattern of Our Days* (p. 50)

Drama

Michael Forster, 'Sunday trading', in *Act One*, Kevin Mayhew, 1996

Music

We trust in you (HTC 446)

Now thank we all our God (HAMNS 205, HON 354)

With loving hands (HTC 106)

Restore, O Lord, the honour of your name (SHF 464)

For I'm building a people of power (SHF 109)

Peace is flowing like a river (SHF 431)

Salvator Mundi (MT1 p. 110)

Come and praise the living God (SHF 59)

Let us be grateful (SHF 321)

Jesus is my friend (BBP 78)

Collect and post communion prayer

Advent 2000 to Advent 2001	Use the collect and post communion prayer for the Eleventh Sunday after Trinity on page 133
Advent 2003 to Advent 2004	

Sunday between 28 August and 3 September

Proper 17

Readings

Continuous

Jeremiah 2.4-13

The Lord asks the Israelites what fault they found in him that they have strayed so far away from him. They have exchanged their glorious inheritance for worthless idols and no longer seek the presence of the Lord.

or Related

Ecclesiasticus 10.12-18

The desertion of the Lord is seen as the first stage of pride. The Lord's judgement will come upon such proud people, overturning even mighty princes and nations and replacing them with the humble and lowly.

or

Proverbs 25.6-7

These proverbs warn against exalting oneself above one's station. Instead of claiming a higher place than you deserve, you should wait to be recognized for your worth.

Hebrews 13.1-8,15-16

The writer teaches on a variety of issues, including our attitudes to strangers, to those in prison and suffering ill-treatment, to the sanctity of marriage, and to money. The writer concludes with an exhortation to offer God praise and to share with others.

Luke 14.1,7-14

While eating at the home of a prominent Pharisee, Jesus notices how the guests pick the places of honour at the table. Jesus proceeds to teach them about humility through a parable about a wedding feast. He tells them that it is better not to take the best places at the feast and face the humiliation of being removed, but to wait until the host has recognized their worth. Jesus then speaks to the Pharisee host, telling him that the invitation to a banquet should be open to all, even the poor and the crippled.

Talk/address/ sermon

Place three different seats in a row at the front – a cushion, a chair and an armchair (or chair decorated in gold foil to look like a throne). Choose three people in turn to come to the front and choose a seat to sit on. Why did they choose that particular seat? What did it feel like to be left only the cushion to sit on (if this happens)?

Discuss the Gospel reading. Do we behave in this manner – at home/church/work? On what occasions do we also seek to better others? What difference should being a Christian make in our attitude towards others?

Congregational/ group activities

- Discuss in small groups: What type of people come to our church? Are there any groups from the local community that aren't properly represented? Why is this? How could this group be made more welcome at church?

- Produce 'Welcome' posters to be displayed outside the church.
- Decorate biscuits and make sweets to be shared with the rest of the congregation at the end of the service.

Prayers/intercessions

Choose a group of people before the service begins. Give each a candle and a prayer, based on one of the themes below. At the time of the intercessions, the group come to the front and lead the prayers. After each has said their prayer they light their candle and use the response:

Leader Lord God, Father of all:

All **help us to remember them.**

Pray for:

- those in prison;
- those suffering difficulties in their marriages;
- those coping with debt;
- those who suffer ill–treatment.

Stories and other resources

'Homelessness' (p. 85), and 'Neighbours' (p. 119), in *Pick and Mix*

Drama

Dave Hopwood, 'The party', in *Acting Up*, NS/CHP, 1995

Paul Powell, 'Partytime', in *Scenes and Wonders*, NS/CHP, 1994

Michael Forster, 'Airs and graces', in *Act Two*, Kevin Mayhew, 1996

Music

Come let us offer a sacrifice of praise (SHF 66)

O accept these words that we bring (SHF 387)

We are here to praise you (SHF 572)

Lord, in your mercy, remember me (WP 72)

Meekness and majesty, manhood and deity (HON 335)

All people that on earth do dwell (HAMNS 100, HON 17, HTC 14)

Lord of all hopefulness, Lord of all joy (HAMNS 394, HON 313, HTC 101)

When morning gilds the skies (HAMNS 146, SHF 603)

Collect and post communion prayer

Advent 2000 to Advent 2001	Use the collect and post communion prayer for the Twelfth Sunday after Trinity on page 134
Advent 2003 to Advent 2004	

Sunday between 4 and 10 September

Proper 18

 ### Readings

Continuous

Jeremiah 18.1-11

Jeremiah watches a potter shaping a pot from clay. On discovering that the clay is marred, he forms it into another pot. The Lord warns Israel that, like the clay in the hand of the potter, so is the house of Israel. They are warned to turn from their evil ways before disaster strikes.

or Related

Deuteronomy 30.15-20

The Lord offers the people of Israel a choice. On the one hand, they will be given life and God's blessing on their land if they follow him. However, if their hearts turn away from him, they will face destruction and their land will be taken from them.

Philemon 1-21

Paul writes from prison to Philemon and other believers in Colossae. He begins by thanking God for their faith in Christ and their love for all the saints. He then appeals for mercy to be shown to Onesimus, who had apparently stolen from Philemon and run away. Paul asks that Onesimus be accepted as a fellow brother in Christ.

Luke 14.25-33

Jesus sets out the uncompromising message that his disciples must love him even more than their own families and be prepared to take up their cross and follow him.

 ### Talk/address/ sermon

Take in a selection of badges or football scarves. Talk about what these badges/scarves represent and how they identify people as belonging to certain groups, with certain beliefs. What are the marks of being a Christian? How would people recognize us as Christians? Show a selection of Christian symbols, such as the cross or the ICHTHUS fish. Why are these symbols important to Christians? What do these tell us about our faith?

 ### Congregational/ group activities

- Make simple thumb pots from clay (roll a small ball of clay, push the thumb into the centre and mould the clay into the shape of a pot).

- Read prayers about faith and what it means to belong to Christ (such as 'After Psalm 19', *The Pattern of Our Days* no. 30). Produce a list of ideas under the title 'Belonging to Christ means . . .'

- Philemon is one of the shortest letters in the Bible. Write letters together in groups. Find out from Amnesty International about those who are wrongly imprisoned and write letters together to the authorities.

- Study Celtic crosses. How did they portray the Christian story on the shape of the cross? Draw a large Celtic cross and decorate with recent stories from the Gospel readings.

- Discuss in small groups: What things can trap and addict us? What are people often trapped by in our local community? What can Jesus free *us* from? How can we show God's power in action to set people free?

Prayers/ intercessions

Use the 'Belonging to Christ' lists that were produced during the group activity as starting points for the prayers.

Use the response:

Leader   Lord of all life

All   **help us to carry your cross.**

Use one of the acts of dedication from *A Church for All Ages*. An example is given below:

Lord God, here are our lives,
Here they are, offered to you.
Given in sadness, given in gladness;
Given for the joy of living, given for the security of
    dying;
Given for determined service on earth, given for ever-
    lasting rest in heaven;
Given because you have loved us from the beginning,
    given because you will love us until the end;
You have the words of eternal life, and we will never
    die,
Lord God, here are our lives,
Here they are for now; here they are forever.

A Church for All Ages (p. 145)

Stories and other resources

Peter Rogers, *From Paul with love . . .*, Hunt & Thorpe, 1996

Books dealing with forms of addiction, such as *Maximus and the TV* by Brian Ogden, Scripture Union, 1996

A Church for All Ages (p. 145)

'Conflict' (p. 35), in *Pick and Mix*

'Words of Faith' in *The Pattern of Our Days* (p. 126)

 ## Music

Let me have my way among you (SHF 312)

Your kingdom come O Lord (WP 84)

You can build a wall around you (CP2 91)

I danced in the morning (HON 228)

You shall go out with joy (HON 571)

Lord Jesus Christ, you have come to us (HAMNS 391, HON 311, HTC 417)

When I survey the wondrous cross (HAMNS 67, HON 549, HTC 147)

Hail to the Lord's anointed (HAMNS 142, HON 193)

Lord of all power, I give you my will (HAMNS 395, HTC 547)

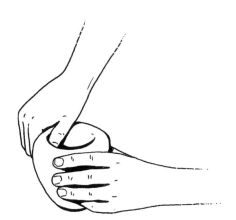

Collect and post communion prayer

Advent 2000 to Advent 2001	Use the collect and post communion prayer for the Thirteenth Sunday after Trinity on page 134
Advent 2003 to Advent 2004	

Sunday between 11 and 17 September

Proper 19

Readings

Continuous

Jeremiah 4.11-12,22-28

Disaster is coming from the north upon Jerusalem and Judah, like a scorching wind from the desert. Jeremiah's vision is a horrifying one of the world returned to primeval chaos – of a formless and empty land lying in ruins.

or Related

Exodus 32.7-14

The Lord's anger is raised against the 'stiff–necked' Israelites for worshipping the idol of the golden calf. Moses intercedes for his people and pleads for the Lord's anger to be turned away from them.

1 Timothy 1.12-17

Paul gives thanks that, even though he was once a blasphemer and persecutor, God's grace was poured out abundantly on him. Through Paul, one of the 'worst of sinners', it is shown that this same mercy and grace is available for all.

Luke 15.1-10

Jesus tells his disciples the parables of the lost sheep and the lost coin. Both these parables show the care taken in searching for what is lost and the great joy in discovering it again. Jesus compares this to the great rejoicing in heaven that occurs when a lost sinner repents.

Talk/address/ sermon

Hide a teddy bear (or other item you might value) somewhere in church. Explain that you have lost something that means a great deal to you. Ask for volunteers to help you hunt for it.

What does it feel like when we lose something very special to us? How do we search for it? How do we feel when we find it? Lead into a discussion of the Gospel reading. What does this passage tell us about God's feelings for us? How does he feel when we return to him?

Congregational/ group activities

- Plan a treasure hunt or scavenger hunt around the church and churchyard.

- Play a simple version of 'Kim's Game'. Place about twenty objects on a tray. Ask the group to close their eyes. Take away several of the objects. Can they work out which ones are missing?

- Make a treasure map or treasure island together. Discuss where the best place might be to hide the treasure.

- Make a banner with the words 'I am the good shepherd'. Produce templates of sheep for children to draw around. Stick different colour wool onto the sheep and put these onto the final banner.

- Begin work on a 'Parables of Jesus' display in church. Ask the congregation to draw a scene from one of the parables, or write a summary of the story. Stick these onto the display.

Prayers/ intercessions

Begin the time of prayer with these responses, adapted from Psalm 51:

Leader   O Lord, open our lips.

All   **And our mouths shall proclaim your praise.**

Leader   You do not delight in prayers offered with hard hearts.

All   **You do not take pleasure in empty prayers or rituals.**

Leader   The sacrifice God accepts is a broken spirit.

All   **He will not turn away from a broken and contrite heart.**

Focus on a time of confession, using this response between the prayers:

Leader   Have mercy on us, O God

All   **according to your unfailing love.**

 ## Stories and other resources

Shirley Hughes, *Hiding*, Walker Books, 1995

'The Lost and Found' flap books, Debbie Tafton O'Neal, *The Lost Coin and The Lost Sheep*, Hunt & Thorpe, 1990

'The lost coin', in *Building New Bridges* (p. 59)

'Losing and finding', in *Under Fives – Alive!* (p. 37)

Drama

Michael Forster, 'What a silly sheep', *Act One*, Kevin Mayhew, 1996

 ## Music

The Lord is my shepherd, I'll follow him always (SLW 108)

We tend our sheep (BBP 34)

God forgave my sin (SHF 126)

I'm forgiven (SHF 189)

God of glory, we exalt your name (SHF 136)

The Lord, the Lord, the Lord is my shepherd (BBP 19)

Thou didst leave thy throne (HAMNS 250, HON 513)

Dear Lord and Father of mankind (HAMNS 115, HTC 356)

Jesus, whose all-redeeming love (HAMNS 383)

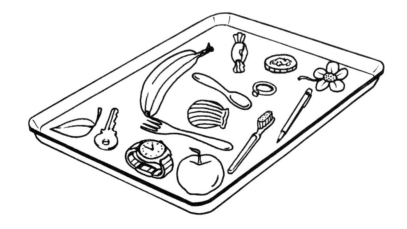

Collect and post communion prayer

Advent 2000 to Advent 2001	Use the collect and post communion prayer for the Fourteenth Sunday after Trinity on page 134
Advent 2003 to Advent 2004	

Sunday between 18 and 24 September

Proper 20

 ### Readings

Continuous

Jeremiah 8.18 – 9.1

The prophet looks with sorrow to the future, when the people of Judah will be taken into exile. He hears the cry of the people, perplexed at why their God has abandoned them. Jeremiah weeps in turn for their fate.

or Related

Amos 8.4-7

The Lord addresses those who trample over the needy and poor in their search for wealth and self–satisfaction. The Lord has seen their dishonesty and will not forget it.

1 Timothy 2.1-7

Paul gives Timothy instructions on worship, urging him to pray for everyone – including those in authority. All need to be prayed for, as God wishes all to be saved and come to a knowledge of the truth.

Luke 16.1-13

Jesus tells the parable of the shrewd manager. A rich man's manager is accused of squandering his master's wealth. The manager decides to call in those who have debts with his master and offer them a reduction, so that they will welcome him with open arms when he is looking for his next job. The master commends the manager for making such shrewd decisions. Jesus teaches that, in the same way, we need to make up our minds astutely about the choices that confront us.

 ### Talk/address/ sermon

Wrap up several presents in advance – some might contain sweets or toys, others junk. Ask some of the congregation to come and choose which present they want to open.

How did they make their choice? What did it feel like to get a useful/useless present?

(Ensure all the unlucky ones are compensated with a good gift before they return to their seats!) Throughout life we make important choices. What are these? How do we choose?

How can our faith help us in making the right choices?

 ### Congregational/ group activities

- In advance, prepare cards with morally right/ wrong/unclear situations on them (such as 'playing football on a Sunday', 'cheating in exams', 'helping with the shopping'). Give each group a selection of the cards. Ask them to group the cards under the categories 'right', 'wrong' or 'either'.

- 'The Moral Maze'. Give each group a series of moral dilemmas to discuss. These might include:

  - you have discovered your best friend cheating at school/work;

  - you find a twenty-pound note on the ground;

  - someone tells you in confidence that they have broken a minor law.

  What course of action would you choose and why?

  Produce some role plays based upon the situations listed above.

- Photocopy simple maze puzzles, or ask groups to produce their own.

Prayers/ intercessions

Choose a selection of people before the service and give them each a prayer focusing on worship. Use this response, adapted from Psalm 113:

Leader From the rising of the sun, to the going down of the same

All **the name of the Lord is to be praised.**

Use the thanksgiving responses in *Patterns for Worship* on pp. 121–5. One of these is printed below:

In my mouth he has put a new song:
praise to our God!
In my mouth he has put a new song:
praise to our God!

I waited patiently upon the Lord;
he stooped to me and heard my cry:
praise to our God!

Many shall see, and stand in awe,
and put their trust in the Lord:
praise to our God!

I love to do your will, Lord God;
your law is deep in my heart:
praise to our God!

I proclaimed righteousness in the great congregation;
behold, I did not restrain my lips:
praise to our God!

Glory to the Father, and to the Son, and to the Holy Spirit.
In my mouth he has put a new song:
praise to our God!

Psalm 40
Patterns for Worship (p. 122)

Stories and other resources

Stories about making hard decisions, such as Barbara Davoll, *A Visit from Rudy Beaver*, Moody, 1996

'Choices', in *Pick and Mix* (p. 31)

Drama

Michael Forster, 'Don't be taken in', *Act One*, Kevin Mayhew, 1996

 ## Music

One more step along the world I go (HON 405)

Will you come and follow me (HON 560)

From the rising of the sun (SHF 121)

From the sun's rising unto the sun's setting (HON 150)

The Lord is my light (HON 486, MT2 p. 73)

All my hope on God is founded (HAMNS 336, HON 15, HTC 451)

Be thou my vision (HAMNS 343, HTC 545)

Thou art the Way: by thee alone (HAMNS 128)

Collect and post communion prayer

Advent 2000 to Advent 2001	Use the collect and post communion prayer for the Fifteenth Sunday after Trinity on page 135
Advent 2003 to Advent 2004	

Sunday between 25 September and 1 October

Proper 21

 ### Readings

Continuous

Jeremiah 32.1-3a,6-15

Jeremiah has been imprisoned by King Zedekiah in the palace courtyard, because he continually prophesies of Judah's downfall at the hands of the Babylonians. Jeremiah buys a field from his uncle, Hanamel. He keeps the deeds of purchase safe in a clay pot, as a sign that after the exile the people will return to reclaim their land.

or Related

Amos 6.1a,4-7

Amos uses vivid language to describe the complacency of the people of Judah and Israel. Their slothfulness is depicted in images of dining on fattened calves and lounging on beds inlaid with ivory. Their fate is foretold and an exile promised where feasting and lounging will end.

1 Timothy 6.6-19

The love of money is seen as the root of all evil, leading people away from faith and into trouble. Paul urges Timothy to stay clear of these temptations and to pursue instead a life of righteousness and faith.

Luke 16.19-31

Jesus tells the parable of the rich man and Lazarus. Lazarus lies covered in sores outside the rich man's gate, but receives no comfort. When he dies, he is taken by the angels to Abraham's side, while the rich man suffers torment in hell after his own death. The rich man requests that Lazarus be sent to warn his five brothers of the fate awaiting them. Abraham replies that if they didn't listen to Moses and the Prophets, they wouldn't listen even to someone rising from the dead.

 ### Talk/address/ sermon

Bring in a black plastic bag full of junk. Empty it out in front of the congregation (preferably onto a plastic sheet, so it can quickly be cleared away).

Talk about the quantity of junk we collect or throw away. Discuss how our society tries to persuade us to keep buying bigger and better products.

How does the message of 1 Timothy challenge us in our own priorities for life? What do we value highest ourselves? What are the temptations facing us that try and persuade us to pursue the love of money?

Lazarus was a social outcast, a piece of 'human junk'. Who are the outcasts in our own society? How highly do we value them?

 ### Congregational/ group activities

* Collect coins (in advance of the service) from different countries. Ask the groups to sort them according to their place of origin. Draw the coins or do coin rubbings.

* Cut out pictures from magazines and group them according to the things we can or cannot buy with money.

* Look at the work of one of the religious orders which takes a vow of poverty.

* Ask each person to draw something they own that is of great value to them, but that others might consider worthless.

* Discuss in small groups: What pressures are put upon us to conform to society and accumulate more and more? In what ways can we support each other in pursuing the life outlined in the Timothy reading?

Prayers/intercessions

Use these words, adapted from Psalm 146, as a basis for the intercessions, praying in turn for each of the named groups:

He upholds the cause of the oppressed and gives food to the hungry . . .

The Lord sets prisoners free, the Lord gives sight to the blind . . .

The Lord lifts up those who are bowed down . . .

The Lord watches over the strangers in a strange land . . .

The Lord sustains the fatherless and the widow . . .

Use this response between each of the prayers:

Leader   Praise the Lord, O my soul.

All   **I will praise the Lord all my life.**

Stories and other resources

Stories about sharing with others, such as Brian Ogden, *Maximus and the Lettuce Thieves*, Scripture Union, 1996

'Junk', in *Pick and Mix* (p. 100)

Music

Change my heart, O God, make it ever true (SHF 53)

If you climb (JU p. 12)

God is so good (JU p. 98)

In my life, Lord, be glorified (SHF 216)

Thank you Jesus (SHF 500)

Fill thou my life, O Lord my God (HAMNS 200, HON 129, HTC 541)

In humble gratitude (HAMNS 377)

What a friend we have in Jesus (HON 541, HTC 373, SHF 598)

Collect and post communion prayer

Advent 2000 to Advent 2001	Use the collect and post communion prayer for the Sixteenth Sunday after Trinity on page 135
Advent 2003 to Advent 2004	

Sunday between 2 and 8 October

Proper 22

 ### Readings

Continuous

Lamentations 1.1-6

A poem of sorrow concerning the desolation of Jerusalem after its destruction in 586 BC and the exile of its people.

or Related

Habakkuk 1.1-4; 2.1-4

Habakkuk rails against God about the injustice, violence and wrongdoing that he sees all around him under the rule of the Babylonians. He protests that evil always seems to overcome righteousness. He then waits on the Lord, who replies to him that there is justice and that life awaits those who are faithful to him.

2 Timothy 1.1-14

Paul writes to Timothy, whom he holds very dear and whose faith he regards as being full of sincerity. He urges Timothy to remember God's gifts to him, to accept the strength so graciously given to him, and to witness shamelessly for the Lord, even if it means suffering.

Luke 17.5-10

This is a reminder that faith can achieve the impossible, and that we should be tireless in living out our faith.

 ### Talk/address/ sermon

The Old Testament readings remind us of the long history of injustice and sadness that has touched every generation. Take a moment to think of something unfair in your own experience, locally, nationally and internationally.

The New Testament readings are about faith, courage and endurance. Are there some real life stories from those for whom this has been a reality?

Faith can bring surprising changes into our lives: those of us who think we are cowards turn out to be strong and courageous; those who feel oppressed find themselves liberated. How can Christians witness to an unjust and pain-ridden world that faith in God changes despair into joy? To what extent does knowledge of God's love lift us above injustice and pain, as it did Paul and Jesus? Is it faith and trust which bring strength to even the most timid?

Those with a joy-filled knowledge of God's love must be constantly reminded of their duty to be channels of that love where there is pain and injustice.

 ### Congregational/ group activities

*   Draw a picture or write a poem about something which is not fair or which is sad. In small groups (of three or four) invite people to talk about their picture, or to read their poem or letter to one another. After each presentation ask the others to respond with their own views. What do they think God would say?

*   Write a letter to God about something which you think is sad or unjust.

- Make a collage from newspapers and magazines of situations which are sad or unjust. If the collage mentioned above has been produced at a mid-week group, display it and invite its creators to talk about it.

- Before the service ask a group of about five people, representing the age groups within the congregation, to watch a video or listen to a tape of a news item describing injustice or sadness. Ask each of them to be prepared to give a 30-second account of their immediate response to it during the service. If God honours our immediate responses as individuals, how might he require us to respond as a church?

- Ask people of different ages who have a story of courage, faith, endurance or liberation if they will share it.

Prayers/ intercessions

Base the intercessions around the following ideas for prayer:

- for those who suffer because of injustice, violence, etc.;

- for confidence in the gifts God has given us – which should be used to the full;

- to identify, acknowledge and thank God for the gifts of others;

- for strength and courage to act for the sake of what is right.

Ask for a poem or letter from the group activities to be read out aloud. Alternatively, ask the congregation to place their pictures (drawn earlier in their groups) on a board at the front of the church. Play or sing some Taizé music while the pictures are being brought up.

Stories and other resources

Christian Aid, Tear Fund, Amnesty International, etc., abound with stories of injustice and ways in which we can respond

Philip Welsh, 'Arnold the 'ard–up aardvark', in *The Reluctant Mole and Other Beastly Tales*, Scripture Union, 1979

Joan Chapman, *Children Celebrate!* (Sections 4, 6, 7, 8, 24), Marshall Pickering, 1994

'Love' (p. 112), and 'Zeal' (p. 182), in *Pick and Mix*

 ## Music

When I'm feeling down and sad (BBP 74)

Inspired by love and anger (HON 252)

O Lord, all the world belongs to you (HON 378)

Alleluia, Alleluia (BBP 43)

We are a kingdom, priesthood to God (SHF 566)

Rock of ages (HAMNS 135, HON 437, HTC 444)

Praise to the holiest in the height (HAMNS 117, HON 426, HTC 140, SHF 450)

O thou who camest from above (HTC 552, SHF 424)

Collect and post communion prayer

Advent 2000 to Advent 2001	Use the collect and post communion prayer for the Seventeenth Sunday after Trinity on page 135
Advent 2003 to Advent 2004	

Sunday between 9 and 15 October

Proper 23

 ### Readings

Continuous

Jeremiah 29.1,4-7

Jeremiah, writing at the time of the exile, encourages God's people to accept their situation and to flourish as a people, despite their captivity.

or Related

2 Kings 5.1-3,7-15c

The story of the faith of humble people (the slave girl and Naaman's servant), and the subsequent cure of the proud Syrian commander by God through Elisha. Naaman's response was to reward Elisha. Elisha declined the offer. Then Naaman gave him what he really desired – the acknowledgement of the God of Israel, and the desire to worship him.

2 Timothy 2.8-15

Paul writes to Timothy about the freedom and hope of the gospel. It is vital not to quibble over unimportant things – stick unashamedly to God's truth for the sake of those who are listening for it.

Luke 17.11-19

Jesus is in the border country. Ten sick men plead for his mercy and he heals them. Only the Samaritan returns to acknowledge him.

 ### Talk/address/ sermon

There is a thread in the Old Testament readings and Epistle related to submitting to situations and trusting God, despite hardship. There may be appropriate stories from South Africa, about the slaves of the USA, about Filipino workers in this country (or even local stories) which relate to this theme. What is meant by words like 'acceptance' and 'submission' as opposed to words like 'resignation' and 'defeat'? What is the reward?

Naaman and the ten men were outcasts because of their leprosy and despised because they were from hated foreign countries (Syria and Samaria respectively). Yet they acknowledged God. What does this say about the surprising places God can be found – and the constraining assumptions that some Christians make about God's activity?

 ### Congregational/ group activities

- Act out the story of Naaman or the story of the ten men. Might the drama be contemporized? Who do we most identify with from the story? Perhaps the story could be told through the eyes of one of the 'minor' characters.

- Reflect on the story of Naaman, drawing out words to describe the characteristics associated with key people emerging at different points in the story, e.g. the slave girl – caring (for Naaman), believing (in Elisha's gifts); Naaman's servant – compassionate (towards his master), wise, challenging, etc.; Naaman – powerful, proud, humble, honourable. Show or face-paint expressions on your faces of these different characteristics. Alternatively, each of the words might be mimed in pairs or threes: a 'still' of compassion, power, etc.

- Christian Aid have produced a video entitled *Together We Stand*. It shows how ordinary people who persevere and hold on to the truth of the gospel can achieve great things for the sake of the kingdom.

- People of all ages choose or draw pictures onto acetates for intercessions.

 ## Prayers/intercessions

These responses are based upon the readings for this Sunday.

Leader	To those who endure hardship the saying is sure:
All	**God remains faithful.**
Leader	To those who avoid petty wrangling the saying is sure:
All	**God remains faithful.**
Leader	To those who pray the saying is sure:
All	**God remains faithful.**
Leader	To those who do not lose heart the saying is sure:
All	**God remains faithful.**
Leader	To those who seek justice the saying is sure:
All	**God remains faithful.**
Leader	To those who rely on God the saying is sure:
All	**God remains faithful.**
Leader	To those who worship God the saying is sure:
All	**God remains faithful.**

Particular situations could be spoken about as they relate to each section.

During these intercessions acetates with pictures drawn or chosen by people of different ages illustrating the themes of the eight petitions could be projected.

 ## Stories and other resources

Peggy Blakeley, *Martin the Cobbler*, A & C Black, 1982

Michael Foreman, *The Two Giants*, Hodder & Stoughton, 1967/1983

'The ten lepers', in *Building New Bridges* (p. 98)

'Conflict', in *Pick and Mix* (p. 35)

 ## Drama

Michael Forster, 'Keep it simple', in *Act Two*, Kevin Mayhew, 1996

 ## Music

Heaven shall not wait (HON 207, WGS1 p. 104)

Christ's is the world in which we move (HON 83)

Keep a light in your eyes (BBP 24)

Praise with joy (WGS1 p. 30)

Caring, sharing (BBP 8)

Now thank we all our God (HAMNS 205, HON 354, HTC 33, SHF 386)

Lord of all hopefulness, Lord of all joy (HAMNS 394, HON 313, HTC 101)

Lead us, heavenly Father, lead us (HAMNS 224, HON 293, HTC 525)

Collect and post communion prayer

Advent 2000 to Advent 2001	**Use the collect and post communion prayer for the Eighteenth Sunday after Trinity on page 136**
Advent 2003 to Advent 2004	

Sunday between 16 and 22 October

Proper 24

 ## *Readings*

Continuous

Jeremiah 31.27-34

God has been with Israel through the bad times. Good times will come and, with them, a new covenant. All will know the forgiveness of God: everyone, 'from the least of them to the greatest' will know his love in their hearts. This 'knowing' will be beyond knowledge as we understand it.

or Related

Genesis 32.22-31

Jacob, still fearful of his brother Esau's wrath years after betraying him, prepares to make his peace. During the night before they meet, and fearful for his and his family's lives at the hands of Esau, he goes to be alone. He meets and wrestles with a man he does not know. The man cannot defeat him, and Jacob will not release him without receiving a blessing. Then he realizes that his wrestling partner is God. With God's blessing upon him and the dawn breaking he goes to face his brother.

2 Timothy 3.14 – 4.5

Paul urges Timothy to remember his childhood teachings and to stand firm in faith, using the Scriptures to equip him for service. Persistence and the teaching of sound doctrine are necessary for the urgent task of proclaiming the gospel. There is no let up – the evangelistic work must be carried out, even if it is a ministry that brings suffering.

Luke 18.1-8

The story of the judge and the persistent widow. Jesus recognizes faith in the woman's constant pleading. Her perception of her own needs and rights, and her belief that the judge will eventually take notice, are a lesson in faith.

 ## *Talk/address/ sermon*

With the Old Testament readings and the Timothy reading in mind:

God is with us through good times and bad – there are times when, like Jacob, we wrestle with God. Sometimes faith is about hanging on to the simplest and most basic of our learning – what is that? Is it different for different people? What tests this learning – leaving home/falling in love/suffering/new ways of thinking? Does it stand the test?

With Timothy in mind:

It is said that we learn the basics of faith as babies, with our primary carers in our homes. In churches the comfort or discomfort of an infant's care has a profound effect upon the child. The early years of learning the faith are very important. Paul recognizes that it is childhood teachings which will sustain Timothy. What should our children be learning? How do they learn it? What are the implications for the Church?

With the Luke reading in mind:

It could be said of the widow that she was a nag! What does that conjure up? What is often peceived as nagging may well be appropriate campaigning for justice. Consider our attitude to charities, human rights movements – are we sometimes inclined to think of them as nagging nuisances? What have been the attitudes to suffragettes, campaigners for the ordination of women, workers who believe themselves to be oppressed, etc.? Are there situations in our own communities or families where we might be misunderstanding a 'nag'?

On the other hand, when does campaigning for justice become misappropriated and sink to selfish whingeing?

Themes in the Genesis reading include: fear, risk and struggle. What is it like to face a friend or member of the family when, like Jacob, you know you have been in the wrong?

Congregational/ group activities

- Make a diagram or draw a picture of your tummy when you are in a similar situation to Jacob – a whirling mass? a host of butterflies? Alternatively, tear out a shape of how you feel. Compose a conversation between the scared you and the brave you before having to face this worrying or embarrassing situation.

- Give each group a sheet of paper. Ask them to write down all the feelings that Jacob must have had before meeting Esau. What do you think or hope was the outcome of their meeting?

- Timothy is urged to remember his childhood teachings. Design a large poster with illustrated statements showing what you have learned about God and Jesus. How would knowing things like this be helpful to Timothy, or indeed anyone?

- Persistence is a theme which seems to run through these readings. Children are often seen as selfishly haranguing to get what they want. Do the children think that this is a correct assumption or do they believe that they are simply persisting for their just deserts, like the widow? What is the difference between selfish wants on the one hand, and rights on the other? An interesting discussion might take place here (perhaps with the help of role play), and may shed light on what Jesus was trying to teach us about God.

- Ask everyone, or representatives from every age group, to say the one most important thing that they have learned about God. Is there someone who can tell a short story about a time of trouble in which their faith sustained them? Can anyone remember someone from childhood who had an influence upon their faith?

Prayers/ intercessions

Have intercessions for causes associated with as many different members of the church as possible, e.g. those who have collected for the Blue Peter Appeal, medical research, the local school, etc. This may involve some preparatory research! Thank God for their efforts and ask God to forgive us when we think we are being nagged!

Use the prayers in the section 'People who help us', from *Prayers for Children* as a basis for prayers for the caring professions.

Stories and other resources

Mercer Mayer, *There's a Nightmare in My Cupboard*, J M Dent and Sons Ltd, 1976

Meryl Doney, *The Very Worried Sparrow*, Lion, 1978

Christopher Herbert, 'People who help us', in *Prayers for Children*, NS/CHP, 1993

The introductions to the chapters on 'St Aidan' (p. 59) and 'St Patrick' (p. 28), in *Seasons, Saints and Sticky Tape*

'Teaching' (p. 159), and 'God' (p. 73), in *Pick and Mix*

'The Persistent Friend', in *Building New Bridges* (p. 62)

Drama

Dave Hopwood, 'The persistent widow', in *A Fistful of Sketches*, NS/CHP, 1996

Music

It's hard to say 'I'm sorry' (BBP 75)

Ask! Ask! Ask and it shall be given you (JP 11)

Oh the word of my Lord (CHE 572)

Ask and it shall be given (SHF 20)

Jesus is my friend (BBP 78)

Lead, kindly light (HAMNS 215, HON 292)

Jesus, good above all other (HAMNS 378, HON 269, HTC 96)

Arise, my soul, arise (SHF 16)

Collect and post communion prayer

Advent 2000 to Advent 2001	Use the collect and post communion prayer for the Nineteenth Sunday after Trinity on page 136
Advent 2003 to Advent 2004	

Sunday between 23 and 29 October

Proper 25

 ### Readings

Continuous

Joel 2.23-32

The prophet exhorts the people to be thankful for what God has done. Even though God sent the destructive locusts, the harvest will be good: he will fill the threshing places and bring reassurance to his people. People of all ages and of every status will proclaim God's message of salvation. Then judgement will come, and all who ask for God's help will be saved.

or Related

Ecclesiasticus 35.12-17

The Lord is not partial. Those of integrity will be heard by him, particularly the poor, the wronged and the grieving. God hears the prayers of all those who serve him. He is a just God.

or

Jeremiah 14.7-10,19-22

This is a 'conversation' between God and his people in which Jeremiah is the mouthpiece. It is a time of terrible drought. The Jews appeal for God's forgiveness of their rejection of him. God tells of his displeasure at their waywardness and his intention to punish them. The people beg God to remember his covenant with them – despite his anger, their only hope is in him.

2 Timothy 4.6-8,16-18

Paul believes he is to die. He is not afraid because he trusts God, who has promised safety in his heavenly kingdom for all who believe in him.

Luke 18.9-14

At the Temple the Pharisee self-righteously relates to God a list of his own virtues: he even reminds God of the inferiority of the tax collector in comparison to him! The tax collector can barely raise his head towards God, so aware is he of his inadequacy before his loving Creator. All he can do is ask for God's pity. Jesus reminds his listeners that it is the humble who are the righteous: those who think too well of themselves have much to learn.

 ### Talk/address/ sermon

Sometimes it is hard to be thankful when life is tough. We can probably identify with the Jews of Jeremiah's time in sometimes thinking God is a stranger. We need to listen for God's message from people of all ages, and we must keep praying in faith because God is there for us.

What is our picture of the kingdom that Paul anticipates with such confidence? In what way is it a place of safety and glory?

What does it mean to be a winner or a success in Christian terms? How do we achieve the balance between wanting to do our best and wanting to be the best?

 ### Congregational/ group activities

- Make a giant 'thank-you' collage of words and pictures cut out from magazines to show those things for which we should remember to thank God.

- Think of situations where there is sadness. Write a poem in the style of the Ecclesiasticus reading to give reassurance to the people in the types of situation you have thought about.

- Paul is looking forward to the safety and glory of God's kingdom. Draw a picture of what you think would be the 'safest' and most 'glorious' place ever. (Include people, places, pets and things.) Thank God for taking notice of what is important to us.

- With the Joel reading in mind, ask individuals or groups from different ages within the church what God's message of salvation is for us. Present this to the congregation in styles which the presenters consider to be appropriate, e.g. a news flash, an advert, a rap, a logo, a story.

- Give out votive candles and ask everyone to pray for one person they know who is sad. Invite everyone to place their candles on the altar or around the cross. When everyone has done so ask a child to say very loudly, 'God hears all our prayers – every one of them!'

 Prayers/ intercessions

Ask the congregation to think of a self-righteous show-off, either at school, work or home. Remember that God loves that person. Ask them to think of the times when they have also acted in this way. Light a candle. Explain how God loves us just as much when we are showing off as when we are humble. Everything we achieve is through God's grace. Say the words of the Grace together. Read out some of the poems written earlier.

Meditate on the 'thank-you' posters that were produced earlier.

Use the Taizé chant 'O Lord hear my prayer, O Lord hear my prayer, when I call, answer me' as a congregational response to specific petitions.

Stories and other resources

Philip Welsh, 'The revenge of Jasper the Toad', in *Ignatius Goes Fishing and More Beastly Tales*, Scripture Union, 1979

Jenny Wagner, *John Brown, Rose and the Midnight Cat*, Penguin, 1997

Robert Munsch, *Giant or Waiting for the Thursday Boat*, Annick Press Ltd, 1989

Terry Jones, 'The three raindrops', in *Fairy Tales*, Puffin, 1981

'Forgiveness' (p. 64), and 'Promises' (p. 139), in *Pick and Mix*

'Harvest', in *Seasons, Saints and Sticky Tape* (p. 62)

 Drama

Michael Forster, 'Representation and reality', in *Act Two*, Kevin Mayhew, 1996

 Music

Thank you, Lord, for this new day (HON 468)

I will enter his gates (HON 236, SHF 252)

In the Lord I'll be ever thankful (Taizé song – HON 250)

I, the Lord of sea and sky (HON 235)

O give thanks to the Lord (WGS2 p. 38)

Jubilate ev'rybody (SHF 303)

Glorious things of thee are spoken (HAMNS 172, HON 158, HTC 494)

Great is thy faithfulness (HON 186, HTC 260)

From all that dwell below the skies (HAMNS 98, HON 146, HTC 580)

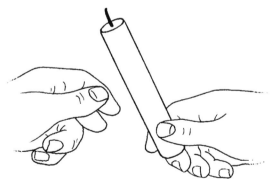

Collect and post communion prayer

Advent 2000 to Advent 2001	**Use the collect and post communion prayer for the Last Sunday after Trinity on page 137**
Advent 2003 to Advent 2004	

Bible Sunday

(Bible Sunday may be celebrated in preference to the provision for the Last Sunday after Trinity)

 ## Readings

Isaiah 45.22-25

God speaks to his people through the prophet, urging them to turn to him and be saved. He is the only God: his promise does not falter. All will come to him and promise loyalty: they will know that only through God can victory and strength be found. God's enemies will be disgraced: the Jews will be saved and will give praise to God.

Romans 15.1-6

The strong in faith should help to build up the faith of the weak. Christians should not please themselves: they should follow the example of Jesus and the teaching of the Scriptures, giving hope through encouragement and patience. Thus everyone will praise God together with one voice.

Luke 4.16-24

Jesus returns to his home town of Nazareth. On the Sabbath he goes to the synagogue where the reading he is given comes from Isaiah. Having read the prophecy he claims that it is he who is chosen by God to bring good news to the poor, liberty to captives, sight to the blind, freedom to the oppressed and the announcement that the time of God's redemption is here. His listeners are impressed until they recognize him as Joseph's son. He remarks that they will not accept him, simply because he is familiar to them.

Collect

Blessed Lord,
who caused all holy scriptures
   to be written for our learning:
help us so to hear them,
to read, mark, learn and inwardly digest them
that, through patience, and the comfort of your
   holy word,
we may embrace and for ever hold fast
   the hope of everlasting life,
which you have given us in our Saviour Jesus Christ,
who is alive and reigns with you,
in the unity of the Holy Spirit,
one God, now and for ever.

 ## Talk/address/ sermon

This ancient book, the Bible – in all the different styles mentioned below – covers thousands of years of the relationship of a people with their God. In it there are expressions of love, sadness, joy, anger, confusion, etc. It is about God's saving activity in the world. If we had to add a book, what form might it take and what would it say about God's work in the world today?

Where do we see the encouragement and patience which Paul regards as vital for the building up of the Church?

Are prophets without honour in our own community or country? Are we missing some vital good news from God now, concerning liberty, sight, freedom and redemption? Are there people right under our noses to whom we should be listening? Use the Bible for discernment.

 ## Congregational/ group activities

- To convey the idea of the Bible as a collection of different types of literature, provide the appropriate number of books (66) and ask the children to build up a 'library'. This idea could be developed by including history/poetry/law/current affairs/biography/religion/story books – and some letters – to show the enormous range of literature held there.

- Make a giant book with three pages. Put in poems, pictures, news reports and stories that depict what is said in each of the readings for today. Look at the finished product together and talk about how the Bible uses lots of different styles to tell of God's work in the world. What do these three pages say to us about God's work?

- Play some co-operative games to demonstrate the importance of working together with encouragement and patience, so that everyone can enjoy being a child of God.

- Ask a child or adult to teach everyone a skill, e.g. how to play a computer game, how to knit, how to do a hair braid, how to change a plug. Reflect on the experience, using the words 'patience' and 'encouragement'. Refer to the Romans reading, then teach everyone a new song of praise – patiently and with encouragement!

- Have fun exploring one of the points in the Luke reading in the following role play. Someone could go around the congregation asking the vicar, churchwardens and church council members whom they rely on. Waffly, pompous answers about insurance companies, employers, the bank could be exaggerated. A child follows the questioner, trying to say something, but is deliberately ignored. Finally and impatiently the child is asked what he or she wants to say. Having answered the question with 'God/Jesus' the child is dismissed with the words: 'Isn't that the child of (name of parents)? Well, I wouldn't take what he/she has to say too literally.' Link this activity with the Gospel reading.

Prayers/ intercessions

Use short silences linked by prayers asking for God to help us listen to him, obey him and encourage others. These might be linked to specific situations. Finish with a hymn or prayer of praise that will be known by everyone.

Select brief biblical extracts about good news, liberty, sight, freedom, God's redemption. Link with current examples of good news, liberty, sight/insight, freedom, God's redemption.

Stories and other resources

Chabert, Marvillier and Galli, *Tell Me the Bible*, Cassell, 1991

Sheila and Charles Front, *Jacob and the Noisy Children*, Andre Deutsch, 1991

Prophets without honour brings to mind Lucy, whom no one believed when she found Narnia: C. S. Lewis, *The Lion, the Witch and the Wardrobe*, HarperCollins 1980 (first published 1950)

'Bible' (p. 18), 'Disciples' (p. 52), 'Love' (p. 112), 'Obedience' (p. 123), in *Pick and Mix*

'All Saints' in *Seasons, Saints and Sticky Tape* (p. 74)

'Jesus' friends', in *Building New Bridges* (p. 81)

Drama

Dave Hopwood, 'The Adrian Puffin show', *A Fistful of Sketches*, NS/CHP, 1996

Music

Jesus put this song into our hearts (HON 275)

He's got the whole world in his hand (HON 206)

Everyone in the whole wide world (JU p. 2)

Cry 'Freedom!' in the name of God (HON 104)

God's Spirit is in my heart (CCH 99)

Thou whose almighty word (HAMNS 180, HON 514, HTC 506)

Help us, O Lord, to learn (HAMNS 373, HTC 493)

God is working his purpose out (HON 172, HTC 188)

Post communion prayer

God of all grace,
your Son Jesus Christ fed the hungry
with the bread of his life
and the word of his kingdom:
renew your people with your heavenly grace,
and in all our weakness
sustain us by your true and living bread;
who is alive and reigns, now and for ever.

Dedication Festival

The first Sunday in October or Last Sunday after Trinity

 ## Readings

1 Chronicles 29.6-19

The Israelite leaders follow King David's example by making gifts of precious metals and stones for the building of a Temple in Jerusalem. The Temple is to be built by David's son, Solomon. David is delighted that God's gifts to his people can be given back in this way – to the glory of God alone, the source of all power. Everything comes from God, so the Temple is not a gift to God; it is the employment of his gifts to his people for his praise. David prays that all will remain faithful and have integrity before God.

Ephesians 2.19-22

It is not only the Jews who are God's people: everyone has a place in the family of God. The foundation of that family has been laid by the prophets and apostles, but the cornerstone is Jesus. When all are in unison with Jesus, the Spirit lives through them, and they are like a temple dedicated to God.

John 2.13-22

Jesus goes to the Temple where preparations and transactions are being made in preparation for the Passover. He is infuriated, violently overturning tables and driving out sacrificial animals. He calls upon the people not to reduce this place, built for his Father's glory, into a market place. His fury reminds the watching disciples of a prophecy concerning passionate devotion to God's house. Jesus tells the Jewish leaders, who want proof of his right to do all this, that if they tear the building down he will rebuild it in three days. This the authorities see as an impossibility, for it took 46 years to build the Temple. Jesus, however, is referring to his own body, or so the disciples think when they remember all of this later, after his death and resurrection.

Collect

Almighty God,
to whose glory we celebrate the dedication
 of this house of prayer:
we praise you for the many blessings
you have given to those who worship you here:
and we pray that all who seek you in this place
 may find you,
and, being filled with the Holy Spirit,
may become a living temple acceptable to you;
through Jesus Christ your Son our Lord,
who is alive and reigns with you,
in the unity of the Holy Spirit,
one God, now and for ever.

 ## Talk/address/ sermon

How do we go about maintaining buildings for the glory of God with integrity? We own nothing: everything we have, including our relationships, our possessions, our occupations, our time, our health, our brains, our skills and talents, all belong to God. Are we looking after them properly?

As a church how can we employ all our gifts for the glory of God? What do we measure our activities against to ensure that we are remaining faithful? What are the characteristics of a Spirit-filled community which is like a temple dedicated to God?

Jesus' anger sounds frightening. Where would we have been in the Temple that day? What would we have felt?

Congregational/ group activities

- Make large drawings of your favourite possessions. Make large gift tags and attach them to your drawings with pieces of string. On the gift tag write the words 'With love from God'.

- Design the building of your dreams. Name some of the precious materials you would use to build, furnish and decorate it. For Solomon this was not a dream, it was a reality. He built the temple of his dreams and dedicated it to God.

- Build a tower of bricks. Which brick would have to be removed in order for the tower to fall? Discerning the will of Jesus is as important as discerning the crucial brick, because unless it acts according to the will of Jesus the Church will get muddled, make mistakes and everything will collapse around it.

- Write down gifts and skills of members of the congregation – people might need each other's help to think of some – on individual pieces of paper, e.g. flower arranging, making us laugh, direct speaking, playing football, listening, keeping accounts, smiling, etc. Display or pile them near the altar. Thank God for them and offer them to God's glory.

- Play Jenga. In this game a tower of wooden blocks is constructed. Each player in turn carefully takes out one block from a lower point in the tower and adds it to the top. Eventually the tower will become unstable and collapse. In the same  way we too can remain stable while a few bricks drop out, but when our togetherness begins to crumble and the crucial 'Jesus brick' is removed, we collapse. Mind, we can be rebuilt again!

- Dramatize the Gospel reading, but change the location from the Temple at Passover to the church at the Christmas Fair. How do we know the difference between making our churches into market places, and honourably raising money for God's work?

Prayers/ intercessions

Say together the offertory prayer from *Common Worship* and then repeat the words from 1 Chronicles 29.11-13, pointing out how we are linked with the ancient peoples of Israel through the words we use so often in our worship.

Thank God for what we are good at, or what we most enjoy doing, remembering that everything we do well can be used to praise God.

Use extracts from *The Prophet*, by Kahlil Gibran (pp. 13–14).

Name some gifts and achievements: ask forgiveness for the times when we think our gifts are simply to our credit and not to that of God.

Stories and other resources

Nick Butterworth and Mick Inkpen, *The House on the Rock*, Marshall Pickering, 1986

Brian Moses, *I Feel Angry*, Wayland, 1993

John Ryan, *Mabel and the Tower of Babel*, Wayland, 1993

Kahlil Gibran, *The Prophet*, Heinemann, 1973

'The Kingdom of God' (p. 104), 'Stewardship' (p. 151), 'Buildings' (p. 22), 'Gifts' (p. 68), in *Pick and Mix*

 ## Music

We are being built into a temple (SHF 567)

We are one, we are family (SHF 576)

Free to serve (WP 21)

We are a chosen people (SHF 565)

The Spirit lives to set us free (CCH 618)

Father, Lord of all creation (CCH 453)

Lord Jesus Christ, you have come to us (HAMNS 391, HTC 417, SHF 342)

Christ is made the sure foundation (HON 76, HTC 559, SHF 54)

Christ is our cornerstone (HAMNS 161, HON 77, HTC 564)

Post communion prayer

Father in heaven,
whose Church on earth is a sign of your heavenly peace,
an image of the new and eternal Jerusalem:
grant to us in the days of our pilgrimage
that, fed with the living bread of heaven,
and united in the body of your Son,
we may be the temple of your presence,
the place of your glory on earth,
and a sign of your peace in the world;
through Jesus Christ our Lord.

Dedication Festival

All Saints' Sunday

Sunday between 30 October and 5 November

All Saints' Day is celebrated on the Sunday between 30 October and 5 November, or if this is not kept as All Saints' Sunday, on 1 November itself. If you wish to use the collects and readings for the Fourth Sunday Before Advent these can be found in *The Christian Year: Calendar, Lectionary and Collects*.

 ## Readings

Daniel 7.1-3,15-18

Daniel describes his vision of four beasts which come out of the sea. He is frightened and wishes to know the meaning of it. A bystander tells him the beasts represent four empires which will arise on earth and that the people of God will receive eternal royal power.

Ephesians 1.11-23

God chooses us to be his people as part of his plan. Through the Holy Spirit we will receive wisdom, knowledge and power; the same power which raised Jesus from the dead and set him as supreme Lord over all things. The Church is likened to Christ's body.

Luke 6.20-31

This is Luke's version of the Sermon on the Mount. Jesus follows this with the injunction to his listeners to do to others only what they would have done to themselves.

Collect

Almighty God,
you have knit together your elect
in one communion and fellowship
   in the mystical body of your Son Christ our
   Lord:
grant us grace so to follow your blessed saints
in all virtuous and godly living
that we may come to those inexpressible joys
that you have prepared for those who truly love
   you;
through Jesus Christ your Son our Lord,
who is alive and reigns with you,
in the unity of the Holy Spirit,
one God, now and for ever.

 ## Talk/address/sermon

Saints are special people, but they are/were real people. 'Sanctity is not so much about hero-worship as about accessibility; the saints are the real men and women of every age in whose lives we can glimpse heaven in our midst. They are our partners in prayer' (*The Promise of His Glory* p. 45). How do we define sainthood in today's culture? How should we use their lives of witness today?

How do we make them relevant? Who are today's saints? What about ourselves, called to be saints, yet we know ourselves as sinners?

Congregational/ group activities

- Find out how the group understands the word 'saint'. How many saints do they know, or can they remember? How many in the group have the same name as a saint? Tell some stories of saints (the list in the Resources section might help you here).

- Make a collage picture of one or more saints, adding their symbols if you know what they are.

- Make stained-glass window pictures of saints using greaseproof paper and wax crayons for the 'glass' parts.

Prayers/ intercessions

Give thanks for saints of every age, for their lives and witness.

Give thanks for local/patronal saints.

Pray for those preaching the gospel, ministering and witnessing in dangerous parts of the world.

Pray for ourselves that we may be given courage and vision to witness for our faith.

Leader God of power and might:

All **give us the courage to speak out.**

Stories and other resources

Philip Welsh, 'Arfa the disgusting camel', in *The Reluctant Mole and Other Beastly Tales*, Scripture Union, 1979

'All Saints', in *Festive Allsorts* (p. 56)

'All Saints', in *Seasons, Saints and Sticky Tape* (p. 74)

'An All Saint-tide presentation of the Christian life', in *Celebration!* (p. 61)

'Communion of Saints', in *The Pattern of Our Days* (p. 157)

Drama

Derek Haylock, 'Tug of war', in *Plays for All Seasons*, NS/CHP, 1997

Ruth Tiller, 'Saints and sinners', in *Keeping the Feast*, Kevin Mayhew, 1995

Derek Haylock, 'Saints alive', in *Plays for All Seasons*, NS/CHP, 1997

Music

I am the church! (BBP 48)

We all march to the beating drum (BBP 76)

We are marching in the light of God (JU p. 34)

We are a kingdom, priesthood to God (SHF 566)

For this purpose Christ was reveal'd (SHF 110)

Rejoice! Rejoice! (SHF 461)

Christ is our cornerstone (HAMNS 161, HON 77, HTC 564)

For all the saints who from their labours rest (HAMNS 305, HON 134, HTC 567)

Let saints on earth in concert sing (HAMNS 182, HON 297, HTC 574)

Post communion prayer

God, the source of all holiness
and giver of all good things:
may we who have shared at this table
as strangers and pilgrims here on earth
be welcomed with all your saints
to the heavenly feast on the day of your kingdom;
through Jesus Christ our Lord.

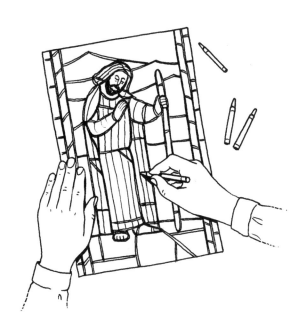

The Third Sunday Before Advent

Sunday between 6 and 12 November

 ## Readings

Job 19.23-27a

Job longs for someone to remember his words. He knows that in spite of all his sufferings, at the last he will see God and God will know who he is.

2 Thessalonians 2.1-5,13-17

The Thessalonians were confused about the Second Coming, believing it had already happened. The letter corrects this and reminds them how they were the first to be called by the saving power of the Holy Spirit; they are urged to remain steady in their faith.

Luke 20.27-38

The Sadducees, who did not believe in resurrection, question Jesus closely about the Law and remarriage. Jesus tells them that the worthy will rise, that Moses believed this and that in God all are alive.

Collect

Almighty Father,
whose will is to restore all things
in your beloved Son, the king of all:
govern the hearts and minds of those in authority,
and bring the families of the nations,
divided and torn apart by the ravages of sin,
to be subject to his just and gentle rule;
who is alive and reigns with you,
in the unity of the Holy Spirit,
one God, now and for ever.

 ## Talk/address/sermon

We know God as King – omnipotent and all-powerful, yet through the Holy Spirit we have a personal relationship with him as our loving Father, as demonstrated in the Job reading. 'In the seventeenth century, the Westminster Assembly defined our purpose as "Man's chief end is to glorify God and enjoy him forever." If we were asked to define the purpose of our lives in one sentence, what might we say?' (*Pick and Mix,* p. 73) Is there a tension between being a subject of the King and a child of the Father?

 ## Congregational/group activities

* How many kings can the group identify? How do we remember them – as good or bad kings? Identify the responsibilities of kingship. What are the qualities of a good king?

* Talk about the symbols of kingship. Make cardboard crowns for everybody. Decorate with pieces of shiny paper or fruit gums for jewels (or use the instructions in *Building New Bridges,* pp. 50–51). *Pick and Mix,* page 12 will tell you how to make orbs and sceptres.

 ## Prayers/ intercessions

Pray for all who rule and govern throughout the world.

Pray for our own royal family and national government.

Pray for all involved in local government; for all those who make decisions on our behalf.

Leader Father, may all who wield power use it well.

All **Give them wisdom and courage.**

The following prayer would be appropriate for any of the services between All Saints' Day and Christ the King.

(We pray for the coming of God's kingdom, saying:
Father, by your Spirit:
bring in your kingdom.)

You came in Jesus to bring good news to the poor,
sight to the blind, freedom to the captives,
and salvation to your people:
anoint us with your Spirit;
rouse us to work in his name.
Father, by your Spirit:
bring in your kingdom.

Send us to bring help to the poor
and freedom to the oppressed.
Father, by your Spirit:
bring in your kingdom.

Send us to tell the world
the good news of your healing love.
Father, by your Spirit:
bring in your kingdom.

Send us to those who mourn,
to bring joy and gladness instead of grief.
Father, by your Spirit:
bring in your kingdom.

Send us to proclaim that the time is here
for you to save your people.

Father, by your Spirit:
bring in your kingdom.

Lord of the Church:
hear our prayer,
and make us one in heart and mind
to serve you with joy for ever. Amen.

Isaiah 61.1-3
Patterns for Worship (pp. 85–6)

 ## Stories and other resources

'David is crowned king', in *Building New Bridges* (p. 49)

'St Oswald', in *Festive Allsorts* (p. 45)

'A king like David', in *Building New Bridges* (pp. 52–3)

Patterns for Worship (pp. 85–6)

 ## Music

King of kings and Lord of lords (SHF 305)

All the kings of the earth (WP 71)

Jesus, remember me (HON 276, MT1 p. 9)

Lift up your heads to the coming King (SHF 328)

There is a Redeemer (HON 500, SHF 534)

Post communion prayer

God of peace,
whose Son Jesus Christ proclaimed the kingdom
and restored the broken to wholeness of life:
look with compassion on the anguish of the world,
and by your healing power
make whole both people and nations;
through our Lord and Saviour Jesus Christ.

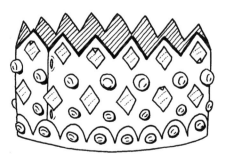

The Second Sunday Before Advent

Sunday between 13 and 19 November

 ## Readings

Malachi 4.1-2a

The prophet foresees the day of judgement and that those who obey God will be saved.

2 Thessalonians 3.6-13

The Thessalonians are urged to work hard as Paul and his followers did when they were with them.

Luke 21.5-19

Jesus speaks of persecution and troubled times ahead. His disciples will be hated and betrayed, but of all those who stand firm, not one will be lost.

Collect

Heavenly Father,
whose blessed Son was revealed
　　to destroy the works of the devil
and to make us the children of God and heirs of
　　eternal life:
grant that we, having this hope,
may purify ourselves even as he is pure;
that when he shall appear in power and great
　　glory
we may be made like him
　　in his eternal and glorious kingdom;
where he is alive and reigns with you,
in the unity of the Holy Spirit,
one God, now and for ever.

Talk/address/sermon

Obedience is a concept Christians struggle with. Not only is it difficult, but unquestioning obedience can bring us into conflict with secular rules and regulations and can deny us the freedom that God has given us. What kind of obedience does Jesus demand? What kind of obedience did he offer God?

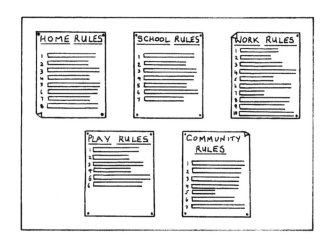

Congregational/ group activities

- Following on from last week's session, recap the main features of kingship and then begin to consider power and ruling. Play 'Simon Says'. Why do we need rules and laws? Identify rules in (a) the home, (b) school, work and play, (c) the community. Make lists of them. Are any the same? Who makes these rules? Who makes us obey, and what happens if we do not?

- What are God's rules? Make a poster or banner to show the message of the two Great Commandments.

# Prayers/ intercessions

Pray for those who make laws.
Pray for those who enforce the law – police, magistrates, traffic wardens, etc.
Pray for ourselves who are subject to the laws of the land and of God.

Leader   Lord of all that is right and just

All   **keep us true to you.**

The following acclamation focuses on the lordship of Jesus Christ:

We praise our ascended and exalted Lord:

Name above every name: Jesus, Lord,
we worship and adore you.

King of righteousness, king of peace,
enthroned at the right hand of Majesty on high:
Jesus, Lord,
we worship and adore you.

Great high priest, advocate with the Father,
living for ever to intercede for us:
Jesus, Lord,
we worship and adore you.

Pioneer of our salvation, bringing many to glory
through your death and resurrection: Jesus, Lord,
we worship and adore you.

**Let every knee bow to you,
and every tongue confess
    that you are Lord,
to the glory of God the Father. Amen.**

Michael Perry, in *Church Family Worship* (no. 303)

Stories and other resources

'Obedience', in *Pick and Mix* (p. 123)

'St Benedict', in *Festive Allsorts* (p. 41)

Church Family Worship (no. 303)

# Music

We are a kingdom, priesthood to God (SHF 566)

Seek ye first the kingdom of God (SHF 471)

Give me joy in my heart (HON 153)

Yours is the kingdom (WP 77)

Praise the name of Jesus (SHF 449)

Jesus is Lord! (HON 270, HTC S17, SHF 278)

When the King shall come again (HTC 200)

Jesus! the name high over all (HTC 213, SHF 294)

Post communion prayer

Gracious Lord,
in this holy sacrament
you give substance to our hope:
bring us at the last
to that fullness of life for which we long;
through Jesus Christ our Saviour.

Christic the King

Sunday between 20 and 26 November (also The Sunday Next Before Advent)

 ## Readings

Jeremiah 23.1-6

The Lord speaks of his anger towards the rulers who have betrayed the interests of his people. He promises to gather his scattered people again and to appoint new rulers who will keep them safe.

Colossians 1.11-20

The reading explains the relationship between Christ and God. Through the powers invested in him by God and his death on the cross, Christ has reconciled to God everything in earth and heaven.

Luke 23.33-43

Jesus is crucified between two thieves. He promises the penitent thief that he will be with him in paradise.

Collect

Eternal Father,
whose Son Jesus Christ ascended to the throne
    of heaven that he might rule over all things as
    Lord and King:
keep the Church in the unity of the Spirit
and in the bond of peace,
and bring the whole created order to worship at
    his feet;
who is alive and reigns with you,
in the unity of the Holy Spirit,
one God, now and for ever.

 ## Talk/address/ sermon

This is the last Sunday of the Church's year. The Old Testament reading tells of God's intention to gather his scattered people, and the promise of a new ruler foreshadows Advent and the coming of the Messiah. It is very difficult to begin to grasp the nature of Christ as both God and man, and to try to make sense of one God revealed as Father, Son and Holy Spirit. It is only by putting the different aspects of Jesus together that we begin to glimpse what he, and through him God, is like. A familiar way of explaining the Trinity is by way of using the example of the three forms of water. Running water is like the life-force of God that created and sustains life itself. The ice is a solid form of water that can be held and touched and is like the incarnated Jesus. The steam is like the Holy Spirit – an invisible but powerful force. All three forms of water – flowing, ice and steam – have the same basic properties, yet different qualities. In the same way the Trinity – God, Jesus, the Holy Spirit – are of the same nature, but have different and distinct qualities.

 ## Congregational/ group activities

* Following on from the last two weeks, remind everyone of the qualities of kingship that were talked about. How are they realized in Jesus? As well as King, he is Friend, Teacher and Healer. See how many stories the group can identify to show examples of these qualities.

* We also know Jesus as Bread of Life (John 6.35), Light of the World (8.12), Vine (15.1), Door (10.7), Good Shepherd (10.11). Talk about and design pictures and/or symbols that illustrate these descriptions. Make a banner or collage of them. This is also 'Stir up Sunday' (see Post communion prayer). You may wish to make reference to this.

Prayers/ intercessions

Leader   Come among us, Jesus
You whom the angels worship
and children welcome

All   **Come Jesus, and meet us here.**

Leader   Come among us, Jesus
You who hurled the stars into space
and shaped the spider's weaving

All   **Come Jesus, and meet us here.**

Leader   Come among us, Jesus
You who walked the long road to
    Bethlehem
and lit a flame that dances forever

All   **Come Jesus, and meet us here.**

Ruth Burgess, in *The Pattern of Our Days*
(no. 1, p. 105)

Stories and other resources

'Ascension', in *Pick and Mix* (p. 10)

'God', in *Pick and Mix* (p. 73)

'Understanding', in *Pick and Mix* (p. 164)

The Pattern of Our Days (no. 1, p. 105)

♫ ♫ ♯♫ ♩♪♫ Music

The King is among us (HON 483, SHF 511)

The King of glory (SHF 512)

Majesty, worship his majesty (HON 327, SHF 358)

Lord Jesus, we enthrone you (SHF 343)

Christus Vincit – Jubilate Coeli (MT1 p. 91)

Jesus shall reign where'er the sun (HAMNS 143, HON 277, HTC 516, SHF 289)

Heavenly hosts in ceaseless worship (HTC 570)

Rejoice, the Lord is King! (HAMNS 139, HON 432, HTC 180)

Let all the world in every corner sing (HAMNS 202, HON 296, HTC 342)

Post communion prayer

Stir up, O Lord,
the wills of your faithful people;
that they, plenteously bringing forth the fruit of
    good works,
may by you be plenteously rewarded;
through Jesus Christ our Lord.

Appendix A

Collects and Post Communion Prayers
Ordinary Time (Before Lent)

The following prayers will be used with the Proper 1, 2 or 3 services. Please see the tables on these Sundays to match the collects and post communion prayers with the correct services.

The Fifth Sunday Before Lent

Collect

Almighty God,
by whose grace alone we are accepted
    and called to your service:
strengthen us by your Holy Spirit
and make us worthy of our calling;
through Jesus Christ your Son our Lord,
who is alive and reigns with you,
in the unity of the Holy Spirit,
one God, now and for ever.

Post communion prayer

God of truth,
we have seen with our eyes
    and touched with our hands the bread of life:
strengthen our faith
that we may grow in love for you and for each other;
through Jesus Christ our Lord.

The Fourth Sunday Before Lent

Collect

O God,
you know us to be set
in the midst of so many and great dangers,
that by reason of the frailty of our nature
we cannot always stand upright:
grant to us such strength and protection
as may support us in all dangers
and carry us through all temptations;
through Jesus Christ your Son our Lord,
who is alive and reigns with you,
in the unity of the Holy Spirit,
one God, now and for ever.

Post communion prayer

Go before us, Lord, in all we do
with your most gracious favour,
and guide us with your continual help,
that in all our works
begun, continued and ended in you,
we may glorify your holy name,
and finally by your mercy receive everlasting life;
through Jesus Christ our Lord.

The Third Sunday Before Lent

Collect

Almighty God,
who alone can bring order
to the unruly wills and passions of sinful humanity:
give your people grace
so to love what you command
and to desire what you promise,
that, among the many changes of this world,
our hearts may surely there be fixed
where true joys are to be found;
through Jesus Christ your Son our Lord,
who is alive and reigns with you,
in the unity of the Holy Spirit,
one God, now and for ever.

Post communion prayer

Merciful Father,
who gave Jesus Christ to be for us the bread of life,
that those who come to him should never hunger:
draw us to the Lord in faith and love,
that we may eat and drink with him
at his table in the kingdom,
where he is alive and reigns, now and for ever.

Appendix B

Collects and Post Communion Prayers Ordinary Time (After Trinity and Before Advent)

The First Sunday After Trinity

Collect

O God,
the strength of all those who put their trust in you,
mercifully accept our prayers
and, because through the weakness of our mortal
    nature
we can do no good thing without you,
grant us the help of your grace,
that in the keeping of your commandments
we may please you both in will and deed;
through Jesus Christ your Son our Lord,
who is alive and reigns with you,
in the unity of the Holy Spirit,
one God, now and for ever.

Post communion prayer

Eternal Father,
we thank you for nourishing us
with these heavenly gifts:
may our communion strengthen us in faith,
build us up in hope,
and make us grow in love;
for the sake of Jesus Christ our Lord.

The Second Sunday After Trinity

Collect

Lord, you have taught us
that all our doings without love are nothing worth:
send your Holy Spirit
and pour into our hearts that most excellent gift of
    love,
the true bond of peace and of all virtues,
without which whoever lives is counted dead before
    you.
Grant this for your only Son Jesus Christ's sake,
who is alive and reigns with you,
in the unity of the Holy Spirit,
one God, now and for ever.

Post communion prayer

Loving Father,
we thank you for feeding us at the supper of your Son:
sustain us with your Spirit,
that we may serve you here on earth
until our joy is complete in heaven,
and we share in the eternal banquet
with Jesus Christ our Lord.

The Third Sunday After Trinity

Collect

Almighty God,
you have broken the tyranny of sin
and have sent the Spirit of your Son into our hearts
    whereby we call you Father:
give us grace to dedicate our freedom to your service,
that we and all creation may be brought
    to the glorious liberty of the children of God;
through Jesus Christ your Son our Lord,
who is alive and reigns with you,
in the unity of the Holy Spirit,
one God, now and for ever.

Post communion prayer

O God, whose beauty is beyond our imagining
and whose power we cannot comprehend:
show us your glory as far as we can grasp it,
and shield us from knowing more than we can bear
until we may look upon you without fear;
through Jesus Christ our Saviour.

The Fourth Sunday After Trinity

Collect

O God, the protector of all who trust in you,
without whom nothing is strong, nothing is holy:
increase and multiply upon us your mercy;
that with you as our ruler and guide
we may so pass through things temporal
that we lose not our hold on things eternal;
grant this, heavenly Father,
for our Lord Jesus Christ's sake,
who is alive and reigns with you,
in the unity of the Holy Spirit,
one God, now and for ever.

Post communion prayer

Eternal God,
comfort of the afflicted and healer of the broken,
you have fed us at the table of life and hope:
teach us the ways of gentleness and peace,
that all the world may acknowledge
the kingdom of your Son Jesus Christ our Lord.

The Fifth Sunday After Trinity

Collect

Almighty and everlasting God,
by whose Spirit the whole body of the Church
    is governed and sanctified:
hear our prayer which we offer for all your faithful people,
that in their vocation and ministry
they may serve you in holiness and truth
to the glory of your name;
through our Lord and Saviour Jesus Christ,
who is alive and reigns with you,
in the unity of the Holy Spirit,
one God, now and for ever.

Post communion prayer

Grant, O Lord, we beseech you,
that the course of this world may be so peaceably
    ordered by your governance,
that your Church may joyfully serve you
    in all godly quietness;
through Jesus Christ our Lord.

The Sixth Sunday After Trinity

Collect

Merciful God,
you have prepared for those who love you
such good things as pass our understanding:
pour into our hearts such love toward you
that we, loving you in all things and above all things,
may obtain your promises,
which exceed all that we can desire;
through Jesus Christ your Son our Lord,
who is alive and reigns with you,
in the unity of the Holy Spirit,
one God, now and for ever.

Post communion prayer

God of our pilgrimage,
you have led us to the living water:
refresh and sustain us
as we go forward on our journey,
in the name of Jesus Christ our Lord.

The Seventh Sunday After Trinity

Collect

Lord of all power and might,
the author and giver of all good things:
graft in our hearts the love of your name,
increase in us true religion,
nourish us with all goodness,
and of your great mercy keep us in the same;
through Jesus Christ your Son our Lord,
who is alive and reigns with you,
in the unity of the Holy Spirit,
one God, now and for ever.

Post communion prayer

Lord God, whose Son is the true vine and the source
    of life,
ever giving himself that the world may live:
may we so receive within ourselves
    the power of his death and passion
that, in his saving cup,
    we may share his glory and be made perfect in his
    love;
for he is alive and reigns, now and for ever.

The Eighth Sunday After Trinity

Collect

Almighty Lord and everlasting God,
we beseech you to direct, sanctify and govern
    both our hearts and bodies
in the ways of your laws
    and the works of your commandments;
that through your most mighty protection, both here
    and ever,
we may be preserved in body and soul;
through our Lord and Saviour Jesus Christ,
who is alive and reigns with you,
in the unity of the Holy Spirit,
one God, now and for ever.

Post communion prayer

Strengthen for service, Lord,
the hands that have taken holy things;
may the ears which have heard your word
    be deaf to clamour and dispute;
may the tongues which have sung your praise
    be free from deceit;
may the eyes which have seen the tokens of your love
    shine with the light of hope;
and may the bodies which have been fed with your
    body
    be refreshed with the fullness of your life;
glory to you for ever.

The Ninth Sunday After Trinity

Collect

Almighty God,
who sent your Holy Spirit
to be the life and light of your Church:
open our hearts to the riches of your grace,
that we may bring forth the fruit of the Spirit
in love and joy and peace;
through Jesus Christ your Son our Lord,
who is alive and reigns with you,
in the unity of the Holy Spirit,
one God, now and for ever.

Post communion prayer

Holy Father,
who gathered us here around the table of your Son
to share this meal with the whole household of God:
in that new world
   where you reveal the fullness of your peace,
gather people of every race and language
   to share in the eternal banquet
   of Jesus Christ our Lord.

The Tenth Sunday After Trinity

Collect

Let your merciful ears, O Lord,
be open to the prayers of your humble servants;
and that they may obtain their petitions
make them to ask such things as shall please you;
through Jesus Christ your Son our Lord,
who is alive and reigns with you,
in the unity of the Holy Spirit,
one God, now and for ever.

Post communion prayer

God of our pilgrimage,
you have willed that the gate of mercy
should stand open for those who trust in you:
look upon us with your favour
that we who follow the path of your will
may never wander from the way of life;
through Jesus Christ our Lord.

The Eleventh Sunday After Trinity

Collect

O God, you declare your almighty power
most chiefly in showing mercy and pity:
mercifully grant to us such a measure of your grace,
that we, running the way of your commandments,
may receive your gracious promises,
and be made partakers of your heavenly treasure;
through Jesus Christ your Son our Lord,
who is alive and reigns with you,
in the unity of the Holy Spirit,
one God, now and for ever.

Post communion prayer

Lord of all mercy,
we your faithful people have celebrated that one true
   sacrifice
   which takes away our sins and brings pardon and
   peace:
by our communion
keep us firm on the foundation of the gospel
and preserve us from all sin;
through Jesus Christ our Lord.

The Twelfth Sunday After Trinity

Collect

Almighty and everlasting God,
you are always more ready to hear than we to pray
and to give more than either we desire or deserve:
pour down upon us the abundance of your mercy,
forgiving us those things of which our conscience is
     afraid
and giving us those good things
     which we are not worthy to ask
but through the merits and mediation
of Jesus Christ your Son our Lord,
who is alive and reigns with you,
in the unity of the Holy Spirit,
one God, now and for ever.

Post communion prayer

God of all mercy,
in this eucharist you have set aside our sins
and given us your healing:
grant that we who are made whole in Christ
may bring that healing to this broken world,
in the name of Jesus Christ our Lord.

The Thirteenth Sunday After Trinity

Collect

Almighty God,
who called your Church to bear witness
that you were in Christ reconciling the world to your-
     self:
help us to proclaim the good news of your love,
that all who hear it may be drawn to you;
through him who was lifted up on the cross,
and reigns with you in the unity of the Holy Spirit,
one God, now and for ever.

Post communion prayer

God our creator,
you feed your children with the true manna,
the living bread from heaven:
let this holy food sustain us through our earthly pilgrim-
     age
until we come to that place
     where hunger and thirst are no more;
through Jesus Christ our Lord.

The Fourteenth Sunday After Trinity

Collect

Almighty God,
whose only Son has opened for us
a new and living way into your presence:
give us pure hearts and steadfast wills
to worship you in spirit and in truth;
through Jesus Christ your Son our Lord,
who is alive and reigns with you,
in the unity of the Holy Spirit,
one God, now and for ever.

Post communion prayer

Lord God, the source of truth and love,
keep us faithful to the apostles' teaching
     and fellowship,
united in prayer and the breaking of bread,
and one in joy and simplicity of heart,
in Jesus Christ our Lord.

The Fifteenth Sunday After Trinity

Collect

God, who in generous mercy sent the Holy Spirit
    upon your Church in the burning fire of your love:
grant that your people may be fervent
    in the fellowship of the gospel
that, always abiding in you,
they may be found steadfast in faith and active in service;
through Jesus Christ your Son our Lord,
who is alive and reigns with you,
in the unity of the Holy Spirit,
one God, now and for ever.

Post communion prayer

Keep, O Lord, your Church,
    with your perpetual mercy;
and, because without you our human frailty cannot but fall,
keep us ever by your help from all things hurtful,
and lead us to all things profitable to our salvation;
through Jesus Christ our Lord.

The Sixteenth Sunday After Trinity

Collect

O Lord, we beseech you mercifully to hear the prayers
    of your people who call upon you;
and grant that they may both perceive and know
    what things they ought to do,
and also may have grace and power
    faithfully to fulfil them;
through Jesus Christ your Son our Lord,
who is alive and reigns with you,
in the unity of the Holy Spirit,
one God, now and for ever.

Post communion prayer

Almighty God,
you have taught us through your Son
that love is the fulfilling of the law:
grant that we may love you with our whole heart
and our neighbours as ourselves;
through Jesus Christ our Lord.

The Seventeenth Sunday After Trinity

Collect

Almighty God,
you have made us for yourself,
and our hearts are restless till they find their rest in
    you:
pour your love into our hearts and draw us to yourself,
and so bring us at last to your heavenly city
where we shall see you face to face;
through Jesus Christ your Son our Lord,
who is alive and reigns with you,
in the unity of the Holy Spirit,
one God, now and for ever.

Post communion prayer

Lord, we pray that your grace
    may always precede and follow us,
and make us continually to be given to all good works;
through Jesus Christ our Lord.

The Eighteenth Sunday After Trinity

Collect

Almighty and everlasting God,
increase in us your gift of faith
that, forsaking what lies behind
and reaching out to that which is before,
we may run the way of your commandments
and win the crown of everlasting joy;
through Jesus Christ your Son our Lord,
who is alive and reigns with you,
in the unity of the Holy Spirit,
one God, now and for ever.

Post communion prayer

We praise and thank you, O Christ, for this sacred
    feast:
for here we receive you,
here the memory of your passion is renewed,
here our minds are filled with grace,
and here a pledge of future glory is given,
when we shall feast at that table where you reign
with all your saints for ever.

The Nineteenth Sunday After Trinity

Collect

O God, forasmuch as without you
we are not able to please you;
mercifully grant that your Holy Spirit
may in all things direct and rule our hearts;
through Jesus Christ your Son our Lord,
who is alive and reigns with you,
in the unity of the Holy Spirit,
one God, now and for ever.

Post communion prayer

Holy and blessed God,
you have fed us with the body and blood of your Son
and filled us with your Holy Spirit:
may we honour you,
not only with our lips
but in lives dedicated to the service
    of Jesus Christ our Lord.

The Twentieth Sunday After Trinity

Collect

God, the giver of life,
whose Holy Spirit wells up within your Church:
by the Spirit's gifts equip us to live the gospel of Christ
    and make us eager to do your will,
that we may share with the whole creation
    the joys of eternal life;
through Jesus Christ your Son our Lord,
who is alive and reigns with you,
in the unity of the Holy Spirit,
one God, now and for ever.

Post communion prayer

God our Father,
whose Son, the light unfailing,
has come from heaven to deliver the world
    from the darkness of ignorance:
let these holy mysteries open the eyes of our under-
    standing
that we may know the way of life,
and walk in it without stumbling;
through Jesus Christ our Lord.

The Twenty-First Sunday After Trinity

Collect

Grant, we beseech you, merciful Lord,
to your faithful people pardon and peace,
that they may be cleansed from all their sins
and serve you with a quiet mind;
through Jesus Christ your Son our Lord,
who is alive and reigns with you,
in the unity of the Holy Spirit,
one God, now and for ever.

Post communion prayer

Father of light,
in whom is no change or shadow of turning,
you give us every good and perfect gift
and have brought us to birth by your word of truth:
may we be a living sign of that kingdom
where your whole creation will be made perfect
    in Jesus Christ our Lord.

The Last Sunday After Trinity

Collect

Blessed Lord,
who caused all holy scriptures
    to be written for our learning:
help us so to hear them,
to read, mark, learn and inwardly digest them
that, through patience, and the comfort of your holy
    word,
we may embrace and for ever hold fast
    the hope of everlasting life,
which you have given us in our Saviour Jesus Christ,
who is alive and reigns with you,
in the unity of the Holy Spirit,
one God, now and for ever.

Post communion prayer

God of all grace,
your Son Jesus Christ fed the hungry
with the bread of his life
and the word of his kingdom:
renew your people with your heavenly grace,
and in all our weakness
sustain us by your true and living bread;
who is alive and reigns, now and for ever.

Collect

O God, forasmuch as without you
we are not able to please you;
mercifully grant that your Holy Spirit
may in all things direct and rule our hearts;
through Jesus Christ your Son our Lord,
who is alive and reigns with you,
in the unity of the Holy Spirit,
one God, now and for ever.

Post communion prayer

Holy and blessed God,
you have fed us with the body and blood of your Son
and filled us with your Holy Spirit:
may we honour you,
not only with our lips
but in lives dedicated to the service
    of Jesus Christ our Lord.